WRIGHT FAMILY

PATENT DEEDS AND LAND GRANTS, 1761-1900; DEED RECORDS, 1761-1903; CHANCERY COURT FILES, 1804-1900; DEATH RECORDS, 1853-1920; CEMETERY RECORDS BY CEMETERY; AND PROBATE RECORDS, 1761-1900

IN

AMHERST COUNTY, VIRGINIA

Robert N. Grant

HERITAGE BOOKS
2009

HERITAGE BOOKS
AN IMPRINT OF HERITAGE BOOKS, INC.

Books, CDs, and more—Worldwide

For our listing of thousands of titles see our website
at
www.HeritageBooks.com

Published 2009 by
HERITAGE BOOKS, INC.
Publishing Division
100 Railroad Ave. #104
Westminster, Maryland 21157

Copyright © 2009 Robert N. Grant

All rights reserved. No part of this book may be reproduced or transmitted in any form or by any means, electronic or mechanical, including photocopying, recording or by any information storage and retrieval system without written permission from the author, except for the inclusion of brief quotations in a review.

International Standard Book Numbers
Paperbound: 978-0-7884-4646-7
Clothbound: 978-0-7884-8163-5

WRIGHT FAMILY

PATENT DEEDS AND LAND GRANTS

1761-1900

AMHERST COUNTY, VIRGINIA

Revised as of July 28, 2007

© 2007, Robert N. Grant
0124(072807)

Introduction To Appendix: Patent Deeds for Amherst County, Virginia

This document is an appendix to a larger work titled Sorting Some Of The Wrights Of Southern Virginia. The work is divided into parts for each family of Wrights that has been researched. Each part is divided into two sections; the first section is text discussing the family and the evidence supporting the relationships and the second section is a descendants chart summarizing the relationships and information known about each individual.

The appendices to the work (of which this document is one) present source records for persons named Wright by county and by type of record with the identification of the person named and their Wright ancestors to the extent known.

The source for the records listed in this appendix is the following:

1) Virginia, Index to Patents 1623-1774, Alphabetically and by Book, microfilm #29308, Genealogical Society of the Church of Jesus Christ of the Latter Day Saints and Patent Deeds available from The Virginia State Library, Richmond, Virginia 23219.

The identification of a person or their ancestor by year and county indicates their year of death and county of residence at death. For example, "1763 Thomas Wright of Bedford County" indicates that this was the Thomas Wright who died in 1763 in Bedford County. If no state is listed after the county, the state is Virginia; counties in states other than Virginia will have a state listed after the county, as in "1876 William S. Wright of Highland County, Ohio".

A parenthetical after the name indicates an identification of the person when a place of death is not yet known, as in "John Wright (Goochland County Carpenter)". A county in parentheses after the name indicates the county with which that person was most identified when no evidence of the place of death has yet been found, as in "Grief Wright (Bedford County)".

All or portions of the text and descendants charts for each Wright family identified are available from the author:

Robert N. Grant
15 Campo Bello Court   (H) 650-854-0895
Menlo Park, California 94025   (O) 650-614-3800

This is a work in progress and I would be most interested in receiving additional information about any of the persons identified in these records in order to correct any errors or expand on the information given.

0124(072807)

Appendix: Amherst County, Virginia, Patent Deeds

Book	Page	Date	Name	Description	Identification
35	187	1763/05/23	William Wright	81 acres on both sides of S. branch of Davis's Creek	William Wright (Amherst County)
36	719	1765/05/14	Menis Wright	190 acres N. side & adjoining Tye River	Parmenos Wright
36	761	1765/06/05	Robert Wright	20 acres on brs. of Davis's Creek under Ragged Mountains	1816 Robert Wright of Nelson County, son of William Wright (Amherst County)
37	126	1767/09/10	Thomas Wright	60 acres on both sides of Ruckers Run	
41	56	1772/08/01	James Wright	63 acres on N. branches of S. fork of Davis's Creek	1839 James Wright of Nelson County, son of William Wright (Amherst County)
16	84	1787/07/10	Arkillis Wright	370 acres on North side of & adjoining Tye River on West side of Berry's Mountain	1825 Achilles Wright of Oldham County, Kentucky
50	267	1802/07/27	Jesse Wright	50 acres on both sides of Mayfield's Creek a branch of Piney River	1850 Jesse Wright of Nelson County, son of 1799 Benjamin Wright of Amherst County and grandson of 1767 Francis Wright of Amherst County
50	269	1802/07/27	Moses Wright	64 acres on Crawley's Creek a branch of Piney River	1830 Moses Wright of Amherst County, son of 1799 Benjamin Wright of Amherst County and grandson of 1767 Francis Wright of Amherst County
59	243	1809/10/10	Benjamin Wright	50 acres on S. waters of Piney River	Benjamin Wright, son of 1830 Moses Wright of Amherst County, grandson of 1799 Benjamin Wright of Amherst County, and great grandson of 1767 Francis Wright of Amherst County

INDEX

Wright, Arkillis, 1
Wright, Benjamin, 1
Wright, James, 1
Wright, Jesse, 1
Wright, Menis, 1
Wright, Moses, 1
Wright, Robert, 1
Wright, Thomas, 1
Wright, William, 1

WRIGHT FAMILY

DEED RECORDS

1761-1903

AMHERST COUNTY, VIRGINIA

Revised as of October 22, 2007

© 2007, Robert N. Grant
0125(102207)

Introduction To Appendix: Deed Records for Amherst County, Virginia

This document is an appendix to a larger work titled Sorting Some Of The Wrights Of Southern Virginia. The work is divided into parts for each family of Wrights that has been researched. Each part is divided into two sections; the first section is text discussing the family and the evidence supporting the relationships and the second section is a descendants chart summarizing the relationships and information known about each individual.

The appendices to the work (of which this document is one) present source records for persons named Wright by county and by type of record with the identification of the person named and their Wright ancestors to the extent known.

The sources for the records listed in this appendix is the following:

1) Amherst County, Virginia, Index of Deeds 1761-1885, microfilm #30283-30284, Genealogical Society of the Church of Jesus Christ of the Latter Day Saints.

2) The Deeds Of Amherst County, Virginia, 1761-1807, And Albemarle County, 1748-1763, by The Rev. Bailey Fulton Davis, Southern Historical Press, c/o The Rev. S. Emmett Lucas, Jr., P.O. Box 738, Easley, South Carolina 29640, 1979.

The identification of a person or their ancestor by year and county indicates their year of death and county of residence at death. For example, "1763 Thomas Wright of Bedford County" indicates that this was the Thomas Wright who died in 1763 in Bedford County. If no state is listed after the county, the state is Virginia; counties in states other than Virginia will have a state listed after the county, as in "1876 William S. Wright of Highland County, Ohio".

A parenthetical after the name indicates an identification of the person when a place of death is not yet known, as in "John Wright (Goochland County Carpenter)". A county in parentheses after the name indicates the county with which that person was most identified when no evidence of the place of death has yet been found, as in "Grief Wright (Bedford County)".

All or portions of the text and descendants charts for each Wright family identified are available from the author:

Robert N. Grant
15 Campo Bello Court   (H) 650-854-0895
Menlo Park, California 94025   (O) 650-614-3800

This is a work in progress and I would be most interested in receiving additional information about any of the persons identified in these records in order to correct any errors or expand on the information given.

0125(051407)

Appendix: Amherst County, Virginia, Deed Records

Book/Page		Date	Grantor	Grantee	Instrument	Identification
A	061	1761/06/07	George Carrington	Isaac Wright	Deed	1807 Isaac Wright of Amherst County, son of 1767 Francis Wright of Amherst County
A	085	1763/03/07	William Wright & Esther Wright	Robert Wright	Deed	Grantor: William Wright (Amherst County) Grantee: 1816 Robert Wright of Nelson County, son of William Wright (Amherst County)
A	185	1764/01/17	John Robinson	Jacob Wright	Deed	1794 Jacob Wright of Laurens County, South Carolina
A	227	1764/07/02	Jacob Wright & Elizabeth Wright	William Harris	Deed	1794 Jacob Wright of Laurens County, South Carolina
B	027	1765/07/01	Menos Wright	Killis Wright	Deed	Grantor: Parmenos Wright Grantee: 1825 Achilles Wright of Oldham County, Kentucky
B	041	1765/07/23	Thomas Wright	John Welch	Deed	
B	276	1767/12/07	Philip Grymes Estate & Mary Grymes & Lunsford Lomax	Augustine Wright	Deed	1776 Augustine Wright of Amherst County
C	104	1768/00/00	Augustine Wright & Alice Wright	Thomas Wilsher	Deed	1776 Augustine Wright of Amherst County
B	327	1768/03/23	William Wright & Esther Wright	James Wright	Deed	Grantor: William Wright (Amherst County) Grantee: 1839 James Wright of Nelson County, son of William Wright (Amherst County)
B	328	1768/03/23	Wm. Wright & Esther Wright	William Hibit	Deed	William Wright (Amherst County)
B	326	1768/03/24	William Wright & Esther Wright	John Wright	Deed	Grantor: William Wright (Amherst County) Grantee: John Wright, son of William Wright (Amherst County)
B	433	1769/06/05	John Woodroof	Thomas Wright	Deed	1793 Thomas Wright of Union District, South Carolina, son of 1767 Francis Wright of Amherst County

Appendix: Amherst County, Virginia, Deed Records

Book/Page		Date	Grantor	Grantee	Instrument	Identification
C	031	1770/02/05	Wm. Burt	Thomas Wright	Gift Assignment of Slaves	Probably 1793 Thomas Wright of Union District, South Carolina, son of 1767 Francis Wright of Amherst County
C	100	1770/08/06	John Rowsa & Mary Rowsa	John Wright	Deed	
C	158	1771/04/01	John Eastains	Benjamin Wright	Deed	1799 Benjamin Wright of Amherst County, son of 1767 Francis Wright of Amherst County
C	278	1771/09/07	Isaac Wright	Peter Carter	Deed	1807 Isaac Wright of Amherst County, son of 1767 Francis Wright of Amherst County
C	272	1772/03/02	James Brown	Benjamin Wright	Deed	1799 Benjamin Wright of Amherst County, son of 1767 Francis Wright of Amherst County.
D	043	1773/01/20	John Loving	Robert Wright & Robert Montgomery & John Johnson & John Tuggle	Mortgage of Personal Property	
D	079	1773/06/05	Geo. Lovell & Elizabeth Lovell	Thomas Wright	Deed	1793 Thomas Wright of Union District, South Carolina, son of 1767 Francis Wright of Amherst County
D	201	1774/01/03	Peter Carter & Maryann Carter	Isaac Wright	Deed	1807 Isaac Wright of Amherst County, son of 1767 Francis Wright of Amherst County
D	148	1774/05/02	Benjamin Wright & Elizabeth Wright	Gabriel Penn	Deed	1799 Benjamin Wright of Amherst County, son of 1767 Francis Wright of Amherst County
D	197	1774/06/06	Deverix Gilliam & Edith Gilliam	Isaac Wright	Deed	1807 Isaac Wright of Amherst County, son of 1767 Francis Wright of Amherst County
D	304	1775/02/01	Jacob Wright & Elizabeth Wright	William Harris	Deed	1794 Jacob Wright of Laurens County, South Carolina

Appendix: Amherst County, Virginia, Deed Records

Book/Page		Date	Grantor	Grantee	Instrument	Identification
D	422	1775/10/22	Isaac Wright	Moses Wright	Deed	Grantor: 1807 Isaac Wright of Amherst County, son of 1767 Francis Wright of Amherst County Grantee: Moses Wright of Adair County, Kentucky, son of 1767 Francis Wright of Amherst County
D	421	1775/10/22	Isaac Wright	Martin Dawson	Deed	1807 Isaac Wright of Amherst County, son of 1767 Francis Wright of Amherst County
D	453	1777/08/17	John Johnston & Dicey Johnston	John Wright	Deed	John Wright, son of William Wright (Amherst County)
E	007	1777/11/06	John Wright & Sarah Wright	Nathaniel Mantiply	Deed	
D	502	1778/03/02	John Wright & Elizabeth Wright	James Halley Burton	Deed	John Wright, son of William Wright (Amherst County)
E	090	1778/11/14	William Morrill	Robert Wright	P A	
E	147	1779/05/17	Wm. Hollandsworth	Killis Wright	Deed	1825 Achilles Wright of Oldham County, Kentucky
E	240	1780/06/05	William Wright Sr. & Esther Wright	Andrew Wright	Deed	Grantor: William Wright (Amherst County) Grantee: 1816 Andrew Wright of Amherst County, son of William Wright (Amherst County)
E	241	1780/06/05	William Wright & Esther Wright	William Wright, Jr.	Deed	Grantor: William Wright (Amherst County) Grantee: William Wright, Jr., son of William Wright (Amherst County)
E	486	1784/03/01	Thomas Wright & Cordelia Wright	John Teneson	Deed	1793 Thomas Wright of Union District, South Carolina, son of 1767 Francis Wright of Amherst County
E	481	1784/03/01	Thomas Wright & Cordelia Wright	John Henry Goodwin	Deed	1793 Thomas Wright of Union District, South Carolina, son of 1767 Francis Wright of Amherst County

Appendix: Amherst County, Virginia, Deed Records

Book/Page		Date	Grantor	Grantee	Instrument	Identification
E	482	1784/03/01	Thomas Wright & Cordelia Wright & John Johnson	John Ward	Deed	1793 Thomas Wright of Union District, South Carolina, son of 1767 Francis Wright of Amherst County
E	546	1784/04/27	Thomas Wright & Cordelo or Dillie Wright	John Miller	Deed	1793 Thomas Wright of Union District, South Carolina, son of 1767 Francis Wright of Amherst County
E	617	1784/09/00	Valentine Payton & Mary Payton	Isaac Wright	Deed	1807 Isaac Wright of Amherst County, son of 1767 Francis Wright of Amherst County
E	613	1784/09/24	Isaac Wright	Vaulintine Payton	Assign of Slave	1807 Isaac Wright of Amherst County, son of 1767 Francis Wright of Amherst County
E	568	1784/11/01	Jos. Edwards & Elloner Edwards	Isaac Wright	Deed	1807 Isaac Wright of Amherst County, son of 1767 Francis Wright of Amherst County
E	611	1784/11/15	Wm. Wright	Robert Wright	Deed	Grantor: William Wright, Jr., son of William Wright (Amherst County) Grantee: 1816 Robert Wright of Nelson County, son of William Wright (Amherst County)
F	038	1785/07/29	Joseph Edwards	Isaac Wright &c	Deed	1807 Isaac Wright of Amherst County, son of 1767 Francis Wright of Amherst County
F	004	1785/08/01	Richard Harrison	Moses Wright	Deed	1830 Moses Wright of Amherst County, son of 1799 Benjamin Wright of Amherst County, and grandson of 1767 Francis Wright of Amherst County
F	027	1785/11/07	William Wright	William Martin & Hudson Martin	Deed	
F	033	1785/12/05	Larkin Gatewood & Cathorine Gatewood	Isaac Wright	Deed	1807 Isaac Wright of Amherst County, son of 1767 Francis Wright of Amherst County
F	045	1786/02/06	Moses Wright & Elizabeth Wright	John Campbell	Deed	1830 Moses Wright of Amherst County, son of 1799 Benjamin Wright of Amherst County and grandson of 1767 Francis Wright of Amherst County

Appendix: Amherst County, Virginia, Deed Records

Book/Page	Date	Grantor	Grantee	Instrument	Identification
F 168	1787/06/04	Robert Wright & Keziah Wright	Samuel Edmonds	Deed	1847 Robert Wright of Madison County, Alabama, son of 1776 Augustine Wright of Amherst County
F 195	1787/07/02	Benjamin Wright & Elizabeth Wright	Nathaniel Hill	Deed	1799 Benjamin Wright of Amherst County, son of 1767 Francis Wright of Amherst County
F 224	1787/08/10	Benjamin Wright	Thompson & Teas	Bill of Sale	1799 Benjamin Wright of Amherst County, son of 1767 Francis Wright of Amherst County
F 198	1787/09/01	Wm. Wright, Sr.	James Wright	Deed	Grantor: William Wright (Amherst County) Grantee: 1839 James Wright of Nelson County, son of William Wright (Amherst County)
F 240	1787/11/30	Isaac Wright and Susannah Wright	Edward Carter	Deed	1807 Isaac Wright of Amherst County, son of 1767 Francis Wright of Amherst County
F 290	1788/11/29	John Wright & Elizabeth Wright	John Loving	Deed	John Wright, son of William Wright (Amherst County)
F 377	1789/08/13	Robert Wright	Joseph Shelton	Deed	1816 Robert Wright of Nelson County, son of William Wright (Amherst County)
F 486	1789/11/28	Moses Wright	Henry Gosney	Deed	Moses Wright of Adair County, Kentucky, son of 1767 Francis Wright of Amherst County
F 510	1790/03/11	Menos Wright	Samuel Edmonds	Deed	Parmenos Wright
F 650	1791/03/10	Benjamin Wright	Jesse Wright	Deed	Grantor: 1799 Benjamin Wright of Amherst County, son of 1767 Francis Wright of Amherst County Grantee: 1850 Jesse Wright of Nelson County, son of 1799 Benjamin Wright of Amherst County and grandson of 1767 Francis Wright of Amherst County

Appendix: Amherst County, Virginia, Deed Records

Book/Page	Date	Grantor	Grantee	Instrument	Identification
F 649	1791/03/10	Benjamin Wright	Jesse Wright	Deed	Grantor: 1799 Benjamin Wright of Amherst County, son of 1767 Francis Wright of Amherst County Grantee: 1850 Jesse Wright of Nelson County, son of 1799 Benjamin Wright of Amherst County and grandson of 1767 Francis Wright of Amherst County
G 184	1792/10/15	Wm. Bibb	Robert Wright & Keziah Wright	Deed	1847 Robert Wright of Madison County, Alabama, son of 1776 Augustine Wright of Amherst County
G 359	1793/10/23	William Houchin	Benjamin Wright	Deed	1799 Benjamin Wright of Amherst County, son of 1767 Francis Wright of Amherst County
G 405	1794/03/08	William Bibb	John Wright & John Alford	Deed	
G 503	1794/03/09	Robert Wright	Wm. Wedderbourn	D T	
G 370	1794/04/21	Isaac Wright & Susanna Wright	John Crawford	Deed	1807 Isaac Wright of Amherst County, son of 1767 Francis Wright of Amherst County
G 363	1794/04/22	Philip Thurmond & Judith Thurmond	Isaac Wright	Deed	1807 Isaac Wright of Amherst County, son of 1767 Francis Wright of Amherst County
G 366	1794/04/22	Isaac Wright & Susanna Wright	Philip Thurmond	Deed	1807 Isaac Wright of Amherst County, son of 1767 Francis Wright of Amherst County
G 491	1794/10/17	Isaac Wright & Susannah Wright	Abraham Carter	Deed	1807 Isaac Wright of Amherst County, son of 1767 Francis Wright of Amherst County
G 523	1795/03/09	Jesse Wright & Robert Wright	James Cocke	Deed	1847 Robert Wright of Madison County, Alabama, son of 1776 Augustine Wright of Amherst County
G 555	1795/07/20	John Wright & Susannah Wright	William Lee Harris	Deed	John Wright, son of 1776 Augustine Wright of Amherst County

Appendix: Amherst County, Virginia, Deed Records

Book/Page		Date	Grantor	Grantee	Instrument	Identification
H	035	1796/07/18	Samuel Edmonds & Alice Edmunds	Menos Wright	Deed	Grantor: Alice or Alcey (Ball) (Wright) Edmunds, former widow of 1776 Augustine Wright of Amherst County Grantee: Parmenos Wright
H	067	1796/09/19	Archilles Wright & Nancy Wright & Young Landrum & Patsey Landrum	Joseph Loving	Deed	1825 Achilles Wright of Oldham County, Kentucky
H	131	1796/11/29	Nancy Wright & Patsey Landrum	Joseph Loving	Relinquishment of Dower	Nancy (____) Wright, wife of 1825 Achilles Wright of Oldham County, Kentucky
H	200	1797/06/17	Isaac Wright & Thomas Goodrich	William Ware	Deed	1807 Isaac Wright of Amherst County, son of 1767 Francis Wright of Amherst County
H	277	1797/10/14	Isaac Wright	Nelson Crawford	Deed	1807 Isaac Wright of Amherst County, son of 1767 Francis Wright of Amherst County
H	276	1797/10/14	Isaac Wright	William Pryor	Deed	1807 Isaac Wright of Amherst County, son of 1767 Francis Wright of Amherst County
H	527	1799/03/11	Menos Wright	James Murphy	D T	Parmenos Wright
I	008	1799/05/18	Jesse Wright, Sr.	James Murphy	D T	Jesse Wright (Amherst County)
I	123	1800/04/28	Jesse Wright, Sr.	James Murphy	D T	Jesse Wright (Amherst County)
I	121	1800/07/15	Menos Wright	James Murphy	D T	Parmenos Wright
I	187	1801/01/17	Isaac Wright & Susannah Wright	Philip Gooch	Deed	1807 Isaac Wright of Amherst County, son of 1767 Francis Wright of Amherst County
I	228	1801/06/08	William Lilly	Isaac Wright	Deed	1807 Isaac Wright of Amherst County, son of 1767 Francis Wright of Amherst County

Appendix: Amherst County, Virginia, Deed Records

Book/Page		Date	Grantor	Grantee	Instrument	Identification
I	273	1801/09/01	John Cartwright	Moses Wright	Deed	1830 Moses Wright of Amherst County, son of 1799 Benjamin Wright of Amherst County and grandson of 1767 Francis Wright of Amherst County
I	316	1801/12/10	William Wright	Esther Wright	Deed	Grantor: William Wright (Amherst County) Grantee: Esther (____) Wright, wife of William Wright (Amherst County)
I	332	1802/01/18	Menos Wright & Elizabeth Wright	Jordan Wright	Deed	Grantor: Parmenos Wright Grantee: 1804 Jordan Wright of Amherst County, son of Parmenos Wright
K	076	1802/03/08	Jordan Wright	James Murphy	D T	1804 Jordan Wright of Amherst County, son of Parmenos Wright
I	385	1802/05/28	Jesse Wright, Jr. & Lindsey Wright	Daniel Higginbotham	D T	Lindsey Wright, son of Jesse Wright (Amherst County)
I	377	1802/06/16	Moses Wright & Elizabeth Wright	John Campbell	Deed	1830 Moses Wright of Amherst County, son of 1799 Benjamin Wright of Amherst County, and grandson of 1767 Francis Wright of Amherst County
I	529	1803/02/10	Richard C. Pollard	John Wright	Deed	Probably John Wright, son of 1816 Robert Wright of Nelson County and grandson of William Wright (Amherst County)
I	565	1803/06/18	James H. Burton	William Wright & Joseph Shelton & Alexander McAlexander	Deed	
K	050	1803/08/02	Elizabeth B. Pollard	John Wright	Rel. of Dower	Probably John Wright, son of 1816 Robert Wright of Nelson County and grandson of William Wright (Amherst County)
K	028	1803/10/29	Robert Wright & Margaret Wright	John Melton	Deed	1816 Robert Wright of Nelson County, son of William Wright (Amherst County)
K	064	1803/11/12	John Wright & Susanna Wright	Parmenus Bryant	Deed	John Wright, son of 1776 Augustine Wright of Amherst County

Appendix: Amherst County, Virginia, Deed Records

Book/Page		Date	Grantor	Grantee	Instrument	Identification
K	249	1804/02/17	Isaac Wright & Susanna Wright	William Ware	Deed	1807 Isaac Wright of Amherst County, son of 1767 Francis Wright of Amherst County
K	188	1804/07/21	John Wright	John Higginbotham	D T	John Wright, son of 1776 Augustine Wright of Amherst County
K	219	1804/08/17	Isaac Wright & Susanna Wright	Abraham Carter	Deed	1807 Isaac Wright of Amherst County, son of 1767 Francis Wright of Amherst County
K	330	1804/11/26	Jesse Wright & Dicey Wright & George Gillaspie & Alexander Gillaspie & Lewis Gillaspie & Sherodmore Gillaspie & James Bowling & Lettie Bowling & Charles Jones & Betsy Jones & Howard Cash & Sally Cash	David S. Garland	Deed	1850 Jesse Wright of Nelson County, son of 1799 Benjamin Wright of Amherst County and grandson of 1767 Francis Wright of Amherst County
K	106	1804/12/11	Jourdan Wright	Jourdan Wright's Parents	Deed	Grantor: 1804 Jordan Wright of Amherst County, son of Parmenos Wright. Grantee: Probably Parmenos Wright
K	299	1805/01/30	Susanna Wright	Parmenos Bryant	Rel. of Dower	Susannah (Bibb) Wright, wife of John Wright, a son of 1776 Augustine Wright of Amherst County
K	307	1805/07/10	Isaac Wright & Susanna Wright	Edward Carter	Deed	1807 Isaac Wright of Amherst County, son of 1767 Francis Wright of Amherst County
K	423	1805/11/13	John Wright	John Higginbotham	D T	John Wright, son of 1776 Augustine Wright of Amherst County
K	491	1806/06/04	Isaac Wright & Susanna Wright	Edward Carter	Com.	1807 Isaac Wright of Amherst County, son of 1767 Francis Wright of Amherst County

Appendix: Amherst County, Virginia, Deed Records

Book/Page		Date	Grantor	Grantee	Instrument	Identification
L	076	1806/07/12	Susanna Wright	William Ware	Rel. of Dower	1807 Isaac Wright of Amherst County, son of 1767 Francis Wright of Amherst County
K	468	1806/09/15	Jesse Wright & John Camden & Thomas Penn	John Campbell	Deed	Probably 1850 Jesse Wright of Nelson County, son of 1799 Benjamin Wright of Amherst County and grandson of 1767 Francis Wright of Amherst County
K	501	1806/10/10	Moses Wright	Benjamin Wright	Deed	Grantor: 1830 Moses Wright of Amherst County, son of 1799 Benjamin Wright of Amherst County and grandson of 1767 Francis Wright of Amherst County Grantee: Benjamin Wright, son of 1830 Moses Wright of Amherst County, grandson of 1799 Benjamin Wright of Amherst County, and great grandson of 1767 Francis Wright of Amherst County
L	065	1807/11/08	Richard C. Pollard & Elizabeth Pollard	John Wright	Deed	John Wright, son of 1816 Robert Wright of Nelson County and grandson of William Wright (Amherst County)
L	267	1809/04/15	Moses Wright	John Campbell	Deed	1830 Moses Wright of Amherst County, son of 1799 Benjamin Wright of Amherst County and grandson of 1767 Francis Wright of Amherst County
L	271	1809/04/15	John Campbell	Moses Wright	Deed	1830 Moses Wright of Amherst County, son of 1799 Benjamin Wright of Amherst County and grandson of 1767 Francis Wright of Amherst County
L	289	1809/07/15	Moses Wright	Benjamin Wright	Deed	Grantor: 1830 Moses Wright of Amherst County, son of 1799 Benjamin Wright of Amherst County and grandson of 1767 Francis Wright of Amherst County Grantee: Benjamin Wright, son of 1830 Moses Wright of Amherst County, grandson of 1799 Benjamin Wright of Amherst County, and great grandson of 1767 Francis Wright of Amherst County
L	335	1810/02/19	Isaac Wright's adm. c.t.a.	William Pryor	Deed	1807 Isaac Wright of Amherst County, son of 1767 Francis Wright of Amherst County
L	333	1810/02/19	Isaac Wright's adm. c.t.a.	John Richeson	Deed	1807 Isaac Wright of Amherst County, son of 1767 Francis Wright of Amherst County

Appendix: Amherst County, Virginia, Deed Records

Book/Page		Date	Grantor	Grantee	Instrument	Identification
L	336	1810/02/19	Isaac Wright's adm. c.t.a.	Richard T. Ellis	Deed	1807 Isaac Wright of Amherst County, son of 1767 Francis Wright of Amherst County
M	376	1813/05/05	Isaac Wright's adm. c.t.a.	William Ware	Deed	1807 Isaac Wright of Amherst County, son of 1767 Francis Wright of Amherst County
M	667	1815/06/17	Robert Wright & Keziah (Gillenwaters) Wright	Elisha Gillenwaters	Deed	Robert Wright, Sr. (Campbell County)
O	554	1817/10/24	William Wright & Cynthia Wright & Joseph Kennedy & Betsy Kennedy & Nunion Wittle & Oney Wittle & William Kelly & Nancy Kelly & John Farrar & Mary Farrar & Wilt(?) Smoot(?) & Susanna Smoot(?) & Jesse Kennedy & Jane Kennedy & Druzilly Kennedy	Joseph Dillard & John London	Deed	1851 William Wright of Amherst County, probably son of William Wright, Jr., and grandson of William Wright (Amherst County)

0125(102207)

11.

Appendix: Amherst County, Virginia, Deed Records

Book/Page	Date	Grantor	Grantee	Instrument	Identification
O 397	1819/10/18	William Wright & Syntha Wright & Joseph Kennedy & Betsy Kennedy & Linion Whittle & Oney Whittle & William Kelly & Nancy Kelly & John Farrar & Mary Farrar & Wiatt Smoot & Susanna Smoot & Jesse Kennedy & Jane Kennedy & John Poindexter & Drusilla Poindexter	Jo. Dillard & Jno London	Deed	1851 William Wright of Amherst County, probably son of William Wright, Jr., and grandson of William Wright (Amherst County)
O 379	1819/12/01	William Wright & Cynthia Wright & Joseph Kennedy & Betsey Kennedy & Ninion Whittle & Oney Whittle & William Kelly & Nancy Kelly & John Farrar & Mary Farrar & Wiatt Smoot & Susanna Smoot & Jesse Kennedy & Jane Kennedy & John Poindexter & Drusilla Poindexter	Jo. Dillard & Jno London	Deed	1851 William Wright of Amherst County, probably son of William Wright, Jr., and grandson of William Wright (Amherst County)
O 592	1820/08/15	John Camden	Jesse Wright	Deed	1850 Jesse Wright of Nelson County, son of 1799 Benjamin Wright of Amherst County and grandson of 1767 Francis Wright of Amherst County

Appendix: Amherst County, Virginia, Deed Records

Book/Page		Date	Grantor	Grantee	Instrument	Identification
O	630	1820/10/09	Stith Mead & Prudence Watkins Mead	Henry Wright	Deed	
P	017	1821/10/29	Joseph Dillard & Judith Dillard	William Wright	Deed	1851 William Wright of Amherst County
O	663	1821/12/21	William Campbell & Frances Campbell	Jesse Wright	Deed	1873 Jesse Wright of Amherst County, son of 1830 Moses Wright of Amherst County, grandson of 1799 Benjamin Wright of Amherst County, and great grandson of 1767 Francis Wright of Amherst County
O	662	1821/12/21	George Campbell & Lucy Campbell	Jesse Wright	Deed	1873 Jesse Wright of Amherst County, son of 1830 Moses Wright of Amherst County, grandson of 1799 Benjamin Wright of Amherst County, and great grandson of 1767 Francis Wright of Amherst County
P	227	1822/11/04	Polly Childress & Robt. & Ab. Crutcher	Thomas Wright	P A	
Q	065	1824/03/08	Moses Wright & Elizabeth Wright	John Campbell	Deed	1830 Moses Wright of Amherst County, son of 1799 Benjamin Wright of Amherst County and grandson of 1767 Francis Wright of Amherst County
Q	321	1825/02/21	Thomas Alfred & Susanna Alfred	William Wright	Deed	1851 William Wright of Amherst County, probably son of William Wright, Jr., and grandson of William Wright (Amherst County)
Q	363	1825/03/03	Thomas Wright	William Armistead	D T	1852 Thomas H. Wright of Bedford County, son of 1810 John Wright of Bedford County and grandson of 1767 Francis Wright of Amherst County
S	091	1827/09/11	John C. Gilbert	John C. Wright	P A	
S	089	1827/11/19	Jesse Wright, Jr.	Sam'l W. Christian	D T	1873 Jesse Wright of Amherst County, son of 1830 Moses Wright of Amherst County, grandson of 1799 Benjamin Wright of Amherst County, and great grandson of 1767 Francis Wright of Amherst County

Appendix: Amherst County, Virginia, Deed Records

Book/Page		Date	Grantor	Grantee	Instrument	Identification
S	123	1828/01/21	William Kelley	William Wright	D T	
S	226	1828/06/00	John Campbell	George G. Wright	P A	George G. Wright, son of 1850 Jesse Wright of Nelson County, grandson of 1799 Benjamin Wright of Amherst County, and great grandson of 1767 Francis Wright of Amherst County
S	255	1828/06/17	Wm. Kelley, Tr.	William Wright	Deed	1851 William Wright of Amherst County, probably son of William Wright, Jr., and grandson of William Wright (Amherst County)
S	226	1828/06/19	James W. Coppedge & Nancy J. Tucker	George G. Wright	P A	George G. Wright, son of 1850 Jesse Wright of Nelson County, grandson of 1799 Benjamin Wright of Amherst County, and great grandson of 1767 Francis Wright of Amherst County
S	335	1828/06/21	David S. Garland Jane H. Garland	Ellis Wright & George G. Wright & Shelton Wright	Deed	1880 Ellis Wright, son of 1850 Jesse Wright of Nelson County, grandson of 1799 Benjamin Wright of Amherst County, and great grandson of 1767 Francis Wright of Amherst County and George G. Wright, son of 1850 Jesse Wright of Nelson County, grandson of 1799 Benjamin Wright of Amherst County, and great grandson of 1767 Francis Wright of Amherst County and 1874 Shelton Wright of Nelson County, son of 1850 Jesse Wright of Nelson County, grandson of 1799 Benjamin Wright of Amherst County, and great grandson of 1767 Francis Wright of Amherst County
S	431	1829/03/14	Lewis Wright	John W. Young	Deed of Trust	1860 Lewis Wright of Lynchburg
S	445	1829/04/28	David S. Garland	Thomas Wright	Deed	1842 Thomas Wright of Buckingham County
T	209	1830/09/20	James S. Martin	Shelton Wright	D T	1874 Shelton Wright of Nelson County, son of 1850 Jesse Wright of Nelson County, grandson of 1799 Benjamin Wright of Amherst County, and great grandson of 1767 Francis Wright of Amherst County
T	234	1830/10/27	Harrison Wright & Permelia Wright	Joseph Wright	Deed	Grantor: 1861 Harrison Wright of Rockbridge County Grantee:

Appendix: Amherst County, Virginia, Deed Records

Book/Page		Date	Grantor	Grantee	Instrument	Identification
T	316	1831/01/18	Henry Wright & Rebecca Wright	Nancy Evans	Deed	
T	336	1831/03/10	William Jackson	William Wright & Moses Philips & Peyton Keith	D T	1851 William Wright of Amherst County, probably son of William Wright, Jr., and grandson of William Wright (Amherst County)
U	310	1833/09/28	Geo. G. Wright	William Wright	Deed	Grantor: George G. Wright, son of 1850 Jesse Wright of Nelson County, grandson of 1799 Benjamin Wright of Amherst County, and great grandson of 1767 Francis Wright of Amherst County Grantee: 1870 William Wright of Amherst County, son of 1850 Jesse Wright of Nelson County, grandson of 1799 Benjamin Wright of Amherst County, and great grandson of 1767 Francis Wright of Amherst County
U	312	1833/12/10	Ellis Wright & George G. Wright & Shelton Wright	Jno. Massie	Deed	1880 Ellis Wright, son of 1850 Jesse Wright of Nelson County, grandson of 1799 Benjamin Wright of Amherst County, and great grandson of 1767 Francis Wright of Amherst County and George G. Wright, son of 1850 Jesse Wright of Nelson County, grandson of 1799 Benjamin Wright of Amherst County, and great grandson of 1767 Francis Wright of Amherst County and 1874 Shelton Wright of Nelson County, son of 1850 Jesse Wright of Nelson County, grandson of 1799 Benjamin Wright of Amherst County, and great grandson of 1767 Francis Wright of Amherst County
U	311	1833/12/10	John Massie Sr.	George G. Wright	D T	George G. Wright, son of 1850 Jesse Wright of Nelson County, grandson of 1799 Benjamin Wright of Amherst County, and great grandson of 1767 Francis Wright of Amherst County
V	410	1836/11/07	John Bonds & William Bonds	William Wright	D T	1870 William Wright, son of 1850 Jesse Wright of Nelson County, grandson of 1799 Benjamin Wright of Amherst County, and great grandson of 1767 Francis Wright of Amherst County
W	109	1837/07/19	Ambrose F. Wright	William C. McAlister	D T	Ambrose F. Wright, son of 1823 George Wright of Campbell County and grandson of Robert Wright, Sr. (Campbell County)

Appendix: Amherst County, Virginia, Deed Records

Book/Page	Date	Grantor	Grantee	Instrument	Identification
W 136	1837/07/20	Benjamin Wright	George G. Wright & William Wright	D T	Grantor: Benjamin Wright, son of 1830 Moses Wright of Amherst County, grandson of 1799 Benjamin Wright of Amherst County, and great grandson of 1767 Francis Wright of Amherst County Grantees: George G. Wright, son of 1850 Jesse Wright of Nelson County, grandson of 1799 Benjamin Wright of Amherst County, and great grandson of 1767 Francis Wright of Amherst County and 1870 William Wright, son of 1850 Jesse Wright of Nelson County, grandson of 1799 Benjamin Wright of Amherst County, and great grandson of 1767 Francis Wright of Amherst County
W 111	1837/07/25	Ambrose F. Wright & John F. Wright & Wm. G. McAllister & John Dillard		Contract	Ambrose F. Wright, son of 1823 George Wright of Campbell County and grandson of Robert Wright, Sr. (Campbell County) and John F. Wright, son of 1823 George Wright of Campbell County and grandson of Robert Wright, Sr. (Campbell County)
W 142	1837/08/19	Ambrose F. Wright	Willis H. Plunkett	D T	Ambrose F. Wright, son of 1823 George Wright of Campbell County and grandson of Robert Wright, Sr. (Campbell County)
W 237	1838/01/22	Benjamin Wright	Wyatt Campbell & Dicey Wright	Deed	Grantor: Benjamin Wright, son of 1830 Moses Wright of Amherst County, grandson of 1799 Benjamin Wright of Amherst County, and great grandson of 1767 Francis Wright of Amherst County Grantee: Dicey (Campbell) Wright, wife of Benjamin Wright, a son of 1830 Moses Wright of Amherst County, grandson of 1799 Benjamin Wright of Amherst County, and great grandson of 1767 Francis Wright of Amherst County
W 502	1838/08/22	Marvel L. Berry	John Wright	Deed	Probably John R. Wright, son of 1877 Joseph Wright of Bedford County

Appendix: Amherst County, Virginia, Deed Records

Book/Page		Date	Grantor	Grantee	Instrument	Identification
W	517	1838/09/17	James Wright & Levicey Wright	James Campbell	Deed	James Wright, son of Benjamin Wright, grandson of 1830 Moses Wright of Amherst County, great grandson of 1799 Benjamin Wright of Amherst County, and great great grandson of 1767 Francis Wright of Amherst County, and Levicey Wright, daughter of Benjamin Wright, granddaughter of 1830 Moses Wright of Amherst County, great granddaughter of 1799 Benjamin Wright of Amherst County, and great great granddaughter of 1767 Francis Wright of Amherst County
W	532	1838/11/17	Thomas Wright & Elizabeth Wright	Jesse Richeson	Deed	1842 Thomas Wright of Buckingham County
W	532	1838/11/19	Jesse Wright	James Campbell	Deed	Jesse Wright, son of Benjamin Wright, grandson of 1830 Moses Wright of Amherst County, great grandson of 1799 Benjamin Wright of Amherst County, and great great grandson of 1767 Francis Wright of Amherst County
W	531	1838/11/20	Charles Wright & Sally Wright	James Campbell	Deed	Charles Wright, son of Benjamin Wright, grandson of 1830 Moses Wright of Amherst County, great grandson of 1799 Benjamin Wright of Amherst County, and great great grandson of 1767 Francis Wright of Amherst County
X	015	1838/12/13	Wiatt Wright	George Wright	P A	Grantor: Wyatt Wright, son of Benjamin Wright, grandson of 1830 Moses Wright of Amherst County, great grandson of 1799 Benjamin Wright of Amherst County, and great great grandson of 1767 Francis Wright of Amherst County Grantee: 1859 George Washington Wright of Gallia County, Ohio, son of Benjamin Wright, grandson of 1830 Moses Wright of Amherst County, great grandson of 1799 Benjamin Wright of Amherst County, and great great grandson of 1767 Francis Wright of Amherst County
X	027	1838/12/13	Wiatt Wright & Eliza Wright & Moses Wright & Ellen Jane Wright & George Wright	James Campbell	Deed	Wyatt Wright and Moses Wright and 1859 George Washington Wright of Gallia County, Ohio, sons of Benjamin Wright, grandsons of 1830 Moses Wright of Amherst County, great grandsons of 1799 Benjamin Wright of Amherst County, and great great grandsons of 1767 Francis Wright of Amherst County

Appendix: Amherst County, Virginia, Deed Records

Book/Page		Date	Grantor	Grantee	Instrument	Identification
X	107	1839/07/29	Jno. Goolsby	William Wright & John F. Camden	D T	1870 William Wright of Amherst County, son of 1850 Jesse Wright of Nelson County, grandson of 1799 Benjamin Wright of Amherst County, and great grandson of 1767 Francis Wright of Amherst County
X	179	1839/09/12	Jesse Wright	George W. Wright	P A	Grantor: Jesse Wright, son of Benjamin Wright, grandson of 1830 Moses Wright of Amherst County, great grandson of 1799 Benjamin Wright of Amherst County, and great great grandson of 1767 Francis Wright of Amherst County Grantee: 1859 George Washington Wright of Gallia County, Ohio, son of Benjamin Wright, grandson of 1830 Moses Wright of Amherst County, great grandson of 1799 Benjamin Wright of Amherst County, and great great grandson of 1767 Francis Wright of Amherst County
X	180	1839/11/18	Levicey W. Right & Rhoda W. Right	George W. Wright	P A	Grantors: Rhoda Wright and Levicey Wright, daughters of Benjamin Wright, granddaughters of 1830 Moses Wright of Amherst County, great granddaughters of 1799 Benjamin Wright of Amherst County, and great great granddaughters of 1767 Francis Wright of Amherst County
X	182	1839/12/16	Rhoda Wright by atty in fact George W. Wright	James Campbell	Deed	Rhoda Wright, daughter of Benjamin Wright, granddaughter of 1830 Moses Wright of Amherst County, great granddaughter of 1799 Benjamin Wright of Amherst County, and great great granddaughter of 1767 Francis Wright of Amherst County
X	261	1840/04/01	Wiatt Campbell	William Wright	D T	1870 William Wright of Amherst County, son of 1850 Jesse Wright of Nelson County, grandson of 1799 Benjamin Wright of Amherst County and great grandson of 1767 Francis Wright of Amherst County
X	320	1840/06/20	Rhoda Wright	James Campbell	Deed	Rhoda Wright, daughter of Benjamin Wright, granddaughter of 1830 Moses Wright of Amherst County, great granddaughter of 1799 Benjamin Wright of Amherst County, and great great granddaughter of 1767 Francis Wright of Amherst County

Appendix: Amherst County, Virginia, Deed Records

Book/Page		Date	Grantor	Grantee	Instrument	Identification
X	345	1840/08/21	Wiatt Wright & Eliza Wright & George Wright & Rachel Wright & Moses Wright & Ellen Jane Wright & Rhoda Wright & Levicy Wright	James Wright	P A	Grantors: Children of Benjamin Wright, grandchildren of 1830 Moses Wright of Amherst County, great grandchildren of 1799 Benjamin Wright of Amherst County, and great great grandchildren of 1767 Francis Wright of Amherst County Grantee: Son of Benjamin Wright, grandson of 1830 Moses Wright of Amherst County, great grandson of 1799 Benjamin Wright of Amherst County, and great great grandson of 1767 Francis Wright of Amherst County
X	483	1841/05/29	William Evans	Ellis Wright	D T	1880 Ellis Wright of Amherst County, son of 1850 Jesse Wright of Nelson County, grandson of 1799 Benjamin Wright of Amherst County, and great grandson of 1767 Francis Wright of Amherst County
X	489	1841/06/25	Benjamin Wright	Hezekiah Jones, Trustee	D T	Benjamin Wright, son of 1830 Moses Wright of Amherst County, grandson of 1799 Benjamin Wright of Amherst County, and great grandson of 1767 Francis Wright of Amherst County
X	535	1841/08/14	Wiatt Campbell	William Wright, Trustee	D T	1870 William Wright of Amherst County, son of 1850 Jesse Wright of Nelson County, grandson of 1799 Benjamin Wright of Amherst County and great grandson of 1767 Francis Wright of Amherst County
Y	083	1841/09/21	Shannon D. Campbell	Ellis Wright, Trustee	D T	1880 Ellis Wright of Amherst County, son of 1850 Jesse Wright of Nelson County, grandson of 1799 Benjamin Wright of Amherst County, and great grandson of 1767 Francis Wright of Amherst County
Y	070	1841/11/25	William Wright	James Higginbotham, Trustee	D T	
Y	105	1842/01/06	Wiatt Campbell Elizabeth Campbell	William Wright, Trustee	D T	1870 William Wright of Amherst County, son of 1850 Jesse Wright of Nelson County, grandson of 1799 Benjamin Wright of Amherst County and great grandson of 1767 Francis Wright of Amherst County

Appendix: Amherst County, Virginia, Deed Records

Book/Page		Date	Grantor	Grantee	Instrument	Identification
Y	107	1842/02/07	Charles Mays	William Wright, Trustee	D T	1870 William Wright of Amherst County, son of 1850 Jesse Wright of Amherst County, grandson of 1799 Benjamin Wright of Amherst County, and great grandson of 1767 Francis Wright of Amherst County
Y	232	1842/08/03	William Wright	Thomas Richeson, Trustee	D T	
Y	438	1843/03/03	William Wright	Rachel S. Wright	D T	Grantor: 1870 William Wright of Amherst County, son of 1850 Jesse Wright of Nelson County, grandson of 1799 Benjamin Wright of Amherst County, and great grandson of 1767 Francis Wright of Amherst County Grantee: Rachel S. (Camden) Wright, wife of 1870 William Wright of Amherst County, son of 1850 Jesse Wright of Nelson County, grandson of 1799 Benjamin Wright of Amherst County, and great grandson of 1767 Francis Wright of Amherst County
Y	482	1843/03/20	William Wright & Rachel S. Wright	John F. Camden	Deed	1870 William Wright of Amherst County, son of 1850 Jesse Wright of Nelson County, grandson of 1799 Benjamin Wright of Amherst County, and great grandson of 1767 Francis Wright of Amherst County
Y	437	1843/03/27	William Wright	John S. Camden	D T	1870 William Wright of Amherst County, son of 1850 Jesse Wright of Nelson County, grandson of 1799 Benjamin Wright of Amherst County, and great grandson of 1767 Francis Wright of Amherst County
Y	511	1843/04/06	Archelaus Gilliam, Jr.	Thomas Wright & Sarah Ann (Gilliam) Wright	Deed	Thomas P. Wright (Lynchburg)
Y	447	1843/04/17	Bransford Mays	Ellis Wright, Trustee	D T	1880 Ellis Wright of Amherst County, son of 1850 Jesse Wright of Nelson County, grandson of 1799 Benjamin Wright of Amherst County, and great grandson of 1767 Francis Wright of Amherst County

Appendix: Amherst County, Virginia, Deed Records

Book/Page		Date	Grantor	Grantee	Instrument	Identification
Z	107	1844/02/22	Henry W. Bird	William Wright & John S. Camden, Trustees	D T	1870 William Wright of Amherst County, son of 1850 Jesse Wright of Nelson County, grandson of 1799 Benjamin Wright of Amherst County and great grandson of 1767 Francis Wright of Amherst County
Z	303	1844/12/28	Daniel A. Nunnelley	Paul C. Wright	Deed	Paul C. Wright, son of 1870 William Wright of Amherst County, grandson of 1850 Jesse Wright of Nelson County, great grandson of 1799 Benjamin Wright of Amherst County, and great great grandson of 1767 Francis Wright of Amherst County
Z	405	1845/08/09	Ellis Wright & Mary P. Wright	Daniel Goode	Deed	1880 Ellis Wright of Amherst County, son of 1850 Jesse Wright of Nelson County, grandson of 1799 Benjamin Wright of Amherst County, and great grandson of 1767 Frances Wright of Amherst County
Z	409	1845/08/18	Ellis Wright	William Wright	D T	Grantor: 1880 Ellis Wright of Amherst County, son of 1850 Jesse Wright of Nelson County, grandson of 1799 Benjamin Wright of Amherst County, and great grandson of 1767 Francis Wright of Amherst County Grantee:
Z	410	1845/08/19	Ellis Wright & Mary P. Wright	William M. Waller	D T	1880 Ellis Wright of Amherst County, son of 1850 Jesse Wright of Nelson County, grandson of 1799 Benjamin Wright of Amherst County, and great grandson of 1767 Frances Wright of Amherst County
Z	479	1845/08/30	James Wright & Eliza A. Wright	Right Wright	Deed	Grantor: 1877 James Wright of Franklin County, son of 1850 Tommey Wright of Bedford County, grandson of 1803 John Wright of Bedford County and great grandson of 1763 Thomas Wright of Bedford County Grantee: 1899 Wright Holland Wright of Bedford County, son of 1841 Matthew Wright of Bedford County, grandson of 1815 Joseph Wright of Bedford County, and great grandson of 1763 Thomas Wright of Bedford County
Z	599	1846/06/12	Charles L. Mitchell & Jno. Mitchell	Thomas Wright	Deed	Thomas P. Wright (Lynchburg)

Appendix: Amherst County, Virginia, Deed Records

Book/Page	Date	Grantor	Grantee	Instrument	Identification
DD 547	1848/07/07	Lewis Wright	Martin D. Tinsely	D.T.	1860 Lewis Wright of Lynchburg
AA 246	1848/08/26	Thomas G. Hill	William Wright	D T	
DD 080	1848/10/07	John F. Camden & Sally Camden	William Wright	Deed	1870 William Wright of Amherst County, son of 1850 Jesse Wright of Amherst County, grandson of 1799 Benjamin Wright of Amherst County, and great grandson of 1767 Francis Wright of Amherst County
CC 490	1855/02/04	John F. Camden	Paul C. Wright	Deed	Paul C. Wright, son of 1870 William Wright of Amherst County, grandson of 1850 Jesse Wright of Nelson County, great grandson of 1799 Benjamin Wright of Amherst County, and great great grandson of 1767 Francis Wright of Amherst County
CC 506	1855/05/20	Henry T. Wright	Samuel M. Garland	D T	1914 Henry Talley Wright of Amherst County, son of William Wright (Hanover County Tailor)
CC 506	1855/05/23	Elijah Fletcher	Henry T. Wright	Deed	1914 Henry Talley Wright of Amherst County, son of William Wright (Hanover County Tailor)
CC 517	1855/05/29	Jesse Wright & Elizabeth Wright	John Cash	Deed	1873 Jesse Wright of Amherst County, son of 1830 Moses Wright of Amherst County, grandson of 1799 Benjamin Wright of Amherst County, and great grandson of 1767 Francis Wright of Amherst County
DD 002	1855/06/02	Jacob Smith & Genova Smith	Charles Wright	Deed	1882 Charles H. Wright of Amherst County, son of Benjamin Wright, grandson of 1830 Moses Wright of Amherst County, great grandson of 1799 Benjamin Wright of Amherst County, and great great grandson of 1767 Francis Wright of Amherst County
DD 043	1855/09/17	Robert Tinsley, Comr	Jesse Wright	Deed	

Appendix: Amherst County, Virginia, Deed Records

Book/Page	Date	Grantor	Grantee	Instrument	Identification
DD 078	1856/01/29	William Wright & Rachel S. Wright	Shelton Wright	D T	Grantor: 1870 William Wright of Amherst County, son of 1850 Jesse Wright of Nelson County, grandson of 1799 Benjamin Wright of Amherst County, and great grandson of 1767 Francis Wright of Amherst County Grantee: 1874 Shelton Wright of Nelson County, son of 1850 Jesse Wright of Nelson County, grandson of 1799 Benjamin Wright of Amherst County, and great grandson of 1767 Francis Wright of Amherst County
DD 094	1856/02/16	William Wright	W. G. Camden	D T	1870 William Wright of Amherst County, son of 1850 Jesse Wright of Amherst County, grandson of 1799 Benjamin Wright of Amherst County, and great grandson of 1767 Francis Wright of Amherst County
DD 538	1857/11/20	Gustavious A. Watts & Elizabeth B. Watts	Shelton H. Wright	Deed	1862 Shelton H. Wright of Amherst County, son of 1873 Jesse Wright of Amherst County, grandson of 1830 Moses Wright of Amherst County, great grandson of 1799 Benjamin Wright of Amherst County, and great great grandson of 1767 Francis Wright of Amherst County
DD 586	1858/01/13	Melonder Wright	Marbell E. Goodwin	Deed	Malinder Wright, son of Benjamin Wright, grandson of 1830 Moses Wright of Amherst County, great grandson of 1799 Benjamin Wright of Amherst County, and great great grandson of 1767 Francis Wright of Amherst County

Appendix: Amherst County, Virginia, Deed Records

Book/Page	Date	Grantor	Grantee	Instrument	Identification
EE 115	1858/08/09	William Wright & Shelton Wright & George Wright & Paul Wright	John F. Camden	Deed	1870 William Wright, son of 1850 Jesse Wright of Nelson County, grandson of 1799 Benjamin Wright of Amherst County, and great grandson of 1767 Francis Wright of Amherst County and 1874 Shelton Wright of Nelson County, son of 1850 Jesse Wright of Nelson County, grandson of 1799 Benjamin Wright of Amherst County, and great grandson of 1767 Francis Wright of Amherst County and George G. Wright, son of 1850 Jesse Wright of Nelson County, grandson of 1799 Benjamin Wright of Amherst County, and great grandson of 1767 Francis Wright of Amherst County and Paul C. Wright, son of 1870 William Wright of Amherst County, grandson of 1850 Jesse Wright of Nelson County, great grandson of 1799 Benjamin Wright of Amherst County, and great great grandson of 1767 Francis Wright of Amherst County
EE 200	1859/01/12	Paul C. Wright	David S. Woodson	D T	Paul C. Wright, son of 1870 William Wright of Amherst County, grandson of 1850 Jesse Wright of Nelson County, great grandson of 1799 Benjamin Wright of Amherst County, and great great grandson of 1767 Francis Wright of Amherst County
EE 213	1859/02/17	Ellis Wright	Geo. Fulcher	D T	1880 Ellis Wright of Amherst County, son of 1850 Jesse Wright of Nelson County, grandson of 1799 Benjamin Wright of Amherst County, and great grandson of 1767 Francis Wright of Amherst County
EE 394	1860/05/21	William P. Wilsher	Shelton H. Wright	Deed	1862 Shelton H. Wright of Amherst County, son of 1873 Jesse Wright of Amherst County, grandson of 1830 Moses Wright of Amherst County, great grandson of 1799 Benjamin Wright of Amherst County, and great great grandson of 1767 Francis Wright of Amherst County

Appendix: Amherst County, Virginia, Deed Records

Book/Page	Date	Grantor	Grantee	Instrument	Identification
FF 055	1861/02/12	Wm. P. Wilcher	Shelton H. Wright	Deed	1862 Shelton H. Wright of Amherst County, son of 1873 Jesse Wright of Amherst County, grandson of 1830 Moses Wright of Amherst County, great grandson of 1799 Benjamin Wright of Amherst County, and great great grandson of 1767 Francis Wright of Amherst County
EE 478	1861/02/12	Shelton H. Wright & Elizabeth Wright	Wm. P. Wilsher	Deed	1862 Shelton H. Wright of Amherst County, son of 1873 Jesse Wright of Amherst County, grandson of 1830 Moses Wright of Amherst County, great grandson of 1799 Benjamin Wright of Amherst County, and great great grandson of 1767 Francis Wright of Amherst County
FF 139	1862/04/22	John F. Camden	William Wright	Deed	1870 William Wright of Amherst County, son of 1850 Jesse Wright of Nelson County, grandson of 1799 Benjamin Wright of Amherst County, and great grandson of 1767 Francis Wright of Amherst County
FF 145	1862/10/27	Henry T. Wright	Lucy F. Smoot & children	Deed	1914 Henry Talley Wright of Amherst County, son of William Wright (Hanover County Tailor)
FF 144	1862/10/27	Sidney Fletcher	Henry T. Wright	Deed	1914 Henry Talley Wright of Amherst County, son of William Wright (Hanover County Tailor)
FF 269	1863/06/04	Jesse Wright & Elizabeth Wright	Lucy Thompson	Deed	1873 Jesse Wright of Amherst County, son of 1830 Moses Wright of Amherst County, grandson of 1799 Benjamin Wright of Amherst County, and great grandson of 1767 Francis Wright of Amherst County
FF 304	1863/08/15	Valerius McGinnis & Mary V. McGinnis	Jesse Wright, Jr.	Deed	
FF 417	1864/05/03	Charles A. Campbell & Nancy Campbell	William Wright	Deed	

Appendix: Amherst County, Virginia, Deed Records

Book/Page	Date	Grantor	Grantee	Instrument	Identification
GG 150	1867/05/30	Charles Wright & Sarah Wright	Dison C. Blanks	Deed	Charles Wright, son of Benjamin Wright, grandson of 1830 Moses Wright of Amherst County, great grandson of 1799 Benjamin Wright of Amherst County, and great great grandson of 1767 Francis Wright of Amherst County
GG 367	1869/01/04	Charles C. Davis & Henrietta C. C. Davis	Philip J. Wright & Camillus Christian	Deed	1903 Phillip James Wright of Richmond City, son of 1853 John Woodson Wright of Cumberland County, grandson of 1838 William Wright of Cumberland County, great grandson of 1774 George Wright of Cumberland County, and great great grandson of 1769 George Wright of Essex County
GG 364	1869/01/28	Phillip J. Wright & Martha H. Wright & Camillus Christian & Mary D. Christian	Samuel B. Christian	Deed	1903 Phillip James Wright of Richmond City, son of 1853 John Woodson Wright of Cumberland County, grandson of 1838 William Wright of Cumberland County, great grandson of 1774 George Wright of Cumberland County, and great great grandson of 1769 George Wright of Essex County
KK 217	1870/01/10	Dicy Wright	Daniel L. Wright	Contract	Grantor: Dicey (Campbell) Wright, widow of Benjamin Wright, a son of 1830 Moses Wright of Amherst County, grandson of 1799 Benjamin Wright of Amherst County, and great grandson of 1767 Francis Wright of Amherst County Grantee: Daniel Lewis Wright, son of Benjamin Wright, grandson of 1830 Moses Wright of Amherst County, great grandson of 1799 Benjamin Wright of Amherst County, and great great grandson of 1767 Francis Wright of Amherst County
HH 347	1870/12/31	Wyatt Tucker & Ellen Tucker	Cary L. Wright	Deed	1914 Cary Lucas "Luke" Wright of Lynchburg, son of 1862 Shelton H. Wright of Amherst County, grandson of 1873 Jesse Wright of Amherst County, great grandson of 1830 Moses Wright of Amherst County, great great grandson of 1799 Benjamin Wright of Amherst County, and great great great grandson of 1767 Francis Wright of Amherst County

Appendix: Amherst County, Virginia, Deed Records

Book/Page	Date	Grantor	Grantee	Instrument	Identification
HH 207	1871/01/09	Charles C. Davis & Henrietta C. C. Davis	Philip J. Wright & Camillus Christian	Release of Lien	1903 Phillip James Wright of Richmond City, son of 1853 John Woodson Wright of Cumberland County, grandson of 1838 William Wright of Cumberland County, great grandson of 1774 George Wright of Cumberland County, and great great grandson of 1769 George Wright of Essex County
HH 266	1871/04/27	William G. Wright	John H. Christian	Deed	William G. Wright, son of 1870 William Wright of Amherst County, grandson of 1850 Jesse Wright of Amherst County, great grandson of 1799 Benjamin Wright of Amherst County, and great great grandson of 1767 Francis Wright of Amherst County
HH 297	1871/05/31	Rachel S. Wright & Martha C. Wright & Sara C. Wright	David S. Woodson	D T	Rachel S. (Camden) Wright, widow of 1870 William Wright of Amherst County, a son of 1850 Jesse Wright of Amherst County, grandson of 1799 Benjamin Wright of Amherst County, and great grandson of 1767 Francis Wright of Amherst County, and her daughters Martha C. Wright and Sarah C. Wright
HH 284	1871/06/03	Paul C. Wright	John H. Christian	Deed	Paul C. Wright, son of 1870 William Wright of Amherst County, grandson of 1850 Jesse Wright of Nelson County, great grandson of 1799 Benjamin Wright of Amherst County, and great great grandson of 1767 Francis Wright of Amherst County
HH 410	1872/02/15	Robert A. Pendleton & Annie S. Pendleton	John W. Wright & Philip J. Wright	Deed	1881 John William Wright of Amherst County, son of 1853 John Woodson Wright of Cumberland County, grandson of 1838 William Wright of Cumberland County, great grandson of 1774 George Wright of Cumberland County, and great great grandson of 1769 George Wright of Essex County and 1903 Phillip James Wright of Richmond City, son of 1853 John Woodson Wright of Cumberland County, grandson of 1838 William Wright of Cumberland County, great grandson of 1774 George Wright of Cumberland County, and great great grandson of 1769 George Wright of Essex County

Appendix: Amherst County, Virginia, Deed Records

Book/Page	Date	Grantor	Grantee	Instrument	Identification
HH 425	1872/02/16	Jno. W. Wright, Philip J. Wright & M. H. Wright	Amelius Christian, Tr.	D T	1881 John William Wright of Amherst County, son of 1853 John Woodson Wright of Cumberland County, grandson of 1838 William Wright of Cumberland County, great grandson of 1774 George Wright of Cumberland County, and great great grandson of 1769 George Wright of Essex County and 1903 Phillip James Wright of Richmond City, son of 1853 John Woodson Wright of Cumberland County, grandson of 1838 William Wright of Cumberland County, great grandson of 1774 George Wright of Cumberland County, and great great grandson of 1769 George Wright of Essex County
JJ 030	1872/06/12	Cary I. Cash & Martha Cash	C. L. Wright	Deed	1914 Cary Lucas "Luke" Wright of Lynchburg, son of 1862 Shelton H. Wright of Amherst County, grandson of 1873 Jesse Wright of Amherst County, great grandson of 1830 Moses Wright of Amherst County, great great grandson of 1799 Benjamin Wright of Amherst County, and great great great grandson of 1767 Francis Wright of Amherst County
JJ 292	1874/04/15	James M. Patteson & Caroline T. Patteson & Benjamin Brown & Sally P. Brown & Robert M. Brown & S. Brown	John W. Wright	Deed	1881 John William Wright of Amherst County, son of 1853 John Woodson Wright of Cumberland County, grandson of 1838 William Wright of Cumberland County, great grandson of 1774 George Wright of Cumberland County, and great great grandson of 1769 George Wright of Essex County
JJ 310	1874/06/10	Philip J. Wright & Martha H. Wright	John W. Wright	Deed	Grantor: 1903 Phillip James Wright of Richmond City, son of 1853 John Woodson Wright of Cumberland County, grandson of 1838 William Wright of Cumberland County, great grandson of 1774 George Wright of Cumberland County, and great great grandson of 1769 George Wright of Essex County Grantee: 1881 John William Wright of Amherst County, son of 1853 John Woodson Wright of Cumberland County, grandson of 1838 William Wright of Cumberland County, great grandson of 1774 George Wright of Cumberland County, and great great grandson of 1769 George Wright of Essex County

Appendix: Amherst County, Virginia, Deed Records

Book/Page	Date	Grantor	Grantee	Instrument	Identification
JJ 351	1874/07/20	Hugh Wright		Homestead Exemption Claim	
KK 087	1875/07/23	Hugh Wright		Homestead Exemption Claim	
PP 227	1876/09/13	R. A. Pendleton	John W. Wright	Plat	1881 John William Wright of Amherst County, son of 1853 John Woodson Wright of Cumberland County, grandson of 1838 William Wright of Cumberland County, great grandson of 1774 George Wright of Cumberland County, and great great grandson of 1769 George Wright of Essex County
NN 337	1876/10/28	C. L. Wright & Rosa E. Wright	Edwin Watson	Deed	1914 Cary Lucas "Luke" Wright of Lynchburg, son of 1862 Shelton H. Wright of Amherst County, grandson of 1873 Jesse Wright of Amherst County, great grandson of 1830 Moses Wright of Amherst County, great great grandson of 1799 Benjamin Wright of Amherst County, and great great great grandson of 1767 Francis Wright of Amherst County
LL 021	1877/06/08	William G. Wright & Paul C. Wright & Rachel S. Wright	David S. Woodson	D T	Rachel S. (Camden) Wright, widow of 1870 William Wright of Amherst County, a son of 1850 Jesse Wright of Nelson County, grandson of 1799 Benjamin Wright of Amherst County, and great grandson of 1767 Francis Wright of Amherst County and Paul C. Wright, son of 1870 William Wright of Amherst County, grandson of 1850 Jesse Wright of Nelson County, great grandson of 1799 Benjamin Wright of Amherst County, and great great grandson of 1767 Francis Wright of Amherst County and William G. Wright, son of 1870 William Wright of Amherst County, grandson of 1850 Jesse Wright of Nelson County, great grandson of 1799 Benjamin Wright of Amherst County, and great great grandson of 1767 Francis Wright of Amherst County
LL 135	1877/09/06	Chas. H. Wright	Geo. Fulcher	B S	

Appendix: Amherst County, Virginia, Deed Records

Book/Page	Date	Grantor	Grantee	Instrument	Identification
LL 102	1878/02/25	Chas. H. Wright	Ro. A. Pendleton	D T	
MM 085	1879/02/07	John W. Wright, Sh'f of Richmond	Henry E. Smith & William P. Terry	Deed	1881 John William Wright of Amherst County, son of 1853 John Woodson Wright of Cumberland County, grandson of 1838 William Wright of Cumberland County, great grandson of 1774 George Wright of Cumberland County, and great great grandson of 1769 George Wright of Essex County
LL 333	1879/03/14	Daniel Lewis Wright, Jr.		Homestead Declaration	Daniel Lewis Wright, son of Benjamin Wright, grandson of 1830 Moses Wright of Amherst County, great grandson of 1799 Benjamin Wright of Amherst County, and great great grandson of 1767 Francis Wright of Amherst County
QQ 035	1879/04/16	Joseph Porter	Fielding H. Wright	Deed	Fielding Hobson Wright, son of 1873 Robert D. Wright of Amherst County, grandson of Charles Wright, and great grandson of Robert Wright, Sr. (Campbell County)
MM 002	1879/08/05	B. E. Wright	W. Dillard Jr., Tr.	Deed	
SS 073	1879/10/23	Robert Isbell & Angelina T. Isbell	Ellen Wright	Deed	Ellen (Hoods) Wright, widow of 1873 Robert D. Wright of Amherst County, a son of Charles Wright, and great grandson of Robert Wright, Sr. (Campbell County)
MM 233	1880/09/20	Burch W. Wright		Homestead Declaration	1905 Burch W. Wright of Amherst County, son of Benjamin Wright, grandson of 1830 Moses Wright of Amherst County, great grandson of 1799 Benjamin Wright of Amherst County, and great great grandson of 1767 Francis Wright of Amherst County
MM 305	1880/11/09	Cary L. Wright & Rosa E. Wright	John H. Christian	Deed	1914 Cary Lucas "Luke" Wright of Lynchburg, son of 1862 Shelton H. Wright of Amherst County, grandson of 1873 Jesse Wright of Amherst County, great grandson of 1830 Moses Wright of Amherst County, great great grandson of 1799 Benjamin Wright of Amherst County, and great great great grandson of 1767 Francis Wright of Amherst County

Appendix: Amherst County, Virginia, Deed Records

Book/Page	Date	Grantor	Grantee	Instrument	Identification
MM 448	1881/03/18	Robert A. Wright & J. W. Healey & S. S. Davidson	Geo. F. Cochnower	Assm't	
NN 052	1881/06/15	Chas. H. Wright		Homestead Declaration	
NN 175	1881/09/10	Thos. G. Tucker & Sarah P. (Wright) Tucker & William J. Tucker & Ann J. (Wright) Tucker	C. L. Wright & W. H. Wright	Deed	1914 Cary Lucas "Luke" Wright of Lynchburg, son of 1862 Shelton H. Wright of Amherst County, grandson of 1873 Jesse Wright of Amherst County, great grandson of 1830 Moses Wright of Amherst County, great great grandson of 1799 Benjamin Wright of Amherst County, and great great great grandson of 1767 Francis Wright of Amherst County and 1914 William Henry Wright of Amherst County, son of 1862 Shelton H. Wright of Amherst County, grandson of 1873 Jesse Wright of Amherst County, great grandson of 1830 Moses Wright of Amherst County, great great grandson of 1799 Benjamin Wright of Amherst County, and great great great grandson of 1767 Francis Wright of Amherst County
NN 206	1881/11/28	Taylor Berry & Martha J. Berry	C. L. Wright & W. H. Wright	Deed	1914 Cary Lucas "Luke" Wright of Lynchburg, son of 1862 Shelton H. Wright of Amherst County, grandson of 1873 Jesse Wright of Amherst County, great grandson of 1830 Moses Wright of Amherst County, great great grandson of 1799 Benjamin Wright of Amherst County, and great great great grandson of 1767 Francis Wright of Amherst County and 1914 William Henry Wright of Amherst County, son of 1862 Shelton H. Wright of Amherst County, grandson of 1873 Jesse Wright of Amherst County, great grandson of 1830 Moses Wright of Amherst County, great great grandson of 1799 Benjamin Wright of Amherst County, and great great great grandson of 1767 Francis Wright of Amherst County

Appendix: Amherst County, Virginia, Deed Records

Book/Page	Date	Grantor	Grantee	Instrument	Identification
NN 318	1882/01/03	William Eggleston & Ella S. Eggleston	C. L. Wright & W. H. Wright	Deed	1914 Cary Lucas "Luke" Wright of Lynchburg, son of 1862 Shelton H. Wright of Amherst County, grandson of 1873 Jesse Wright of Amherst County, great grandson of 1830 Moses Wright of Amherst County, great great grandson of 1799 Benjamin Wright of Amherst County, and great great great grandson of 1767 Francis Wright of Amherst County and 1914 William Henry Wright of Amherst County, son of 1862 Shelton H. Wright of Amherst County, grandson of 1873 Jesse Wright of Amherst County, great grandson of 1830 Moses Wright of Amherst County, great great grandson of 1799 Benjamin Wright of Amherst County, and great great great grandson of 1767 Francis Wright of Amherst County
NN 271	1882/01/23	Jno. D. Hudson & Elizabeth W. Hudson	C. L. Wright & W. H. Wright	Deed	1914 Cary Lucas "Luke" Wright of Lynchburg, son of 1862 Shelton H. Wright of Amherst County, grandson of 1873 Jesse Wright of Amherst County, great grandson of 1830 Moses Wright of Amherst County, great great grandson of 1799 Benjamin Wright of Amherst County, and great great great grandson of 1767 Francis Wright of Amherst County and 1914 William Henry Wright of Amherst County, son of 1862 Shelton H. Wright of Amherst County, grandson of 1873 Jesse Wright of Amherst County, great grandson of 1830 Moses Wright of Amherst County, great great grandson of 1799 Benjamin Wright of Amherst County, and great great great grandson of 1767 Francis Wright of Amherst County
NN 306	1882/04/29	Amelius Christian, Tr.	Jno. W. Wright & Philip J. Wright	R D	1881 John William Wright of Amherst County, son of 1853 John Woodson Wright of Cumberland County, grandson of 1838 William Wright of Cumberland County, great grandson of 1774 George Wright of Cumberland County, and great great grandson of 1769 George Wright of Essex County and 1903 Phillip James Wright of Richmond City, son of 1853 John Woodson Wright of Cumberland County, grandson of 1838 William Wright of Cumberland County, great grandson of 1774 George Wright of Cumberland County, and great great grandson of 1769 George Wright of Essex County

Appendix: Amherst County, Virginia, Deed Records

Book/Page	Date	Grantor	Grantee	Instrument	Identification
NN 432	1882/06/09	James M. Patterson & Caroline T. Patterson & Benjamin Brown & Sally P. Brown & Robert M. Brown & S. A. Brown	John W. Wright	R D	1881 John William Wright of Amherst County, son of 1853 John Woodson Wright of Cumberland County, grandson of 1838 William Wright of Cumberland County, great grandson of 1774 George Wright of Cumberland County, and great great grandson of 1769 George Wright of Essex County
NN 437	1882/10/26	M. H. Miller	Charles H. Wright, Tr.	Deed	Charles H. Wright, son of 1849 Moses Wright of Nelson County, grandson of 1830 Moses Wright of Amherst County, great grandson of 1799 Benjamin Wright of Amherst County, and great great grandson of 1767 Francis Wright of Amherst County
NN 438	1882/11/20	Chas. H. Wright & Mary J. Wright	Wm. G. Loving, Tr.	D T	Charles H. Wright, son of 1849 Moses Wright of Nelson County, grandson of 1830 Moses Wright of Amherst County, great grandson of 1799 Benjamin Wright of Amherst County, and great great grandson of 1767 Francis Wright of Amherst County, and Mary Jane (Wright) Wright, daughter of 1873 Jesse Wright of Amherst County, granddaughter of 1830 Moses Wright of Amherst County, great granddaughter of 1799 Benjamin Wright of Amherst County, and great great granddaughter of 1767 Francis Wright of Amherst County
OO 207	1883/01/22	Samuel W. Brockman & Susan Brockman & & Maria Penn's Exr & Lucy M. Penn & Wm. G. Loving, Comr.	C. L. Wright & W. Henry Wright	Deed	1914 Cary Lucas "Luke" Wright of Lynchburg, son of 1862 Shelton H. Wright of Amherst County, grandson of 1873 Jesse Wright of Amherst County, great grandson of 1830 Moses Wright of Amherst County, great great grandson of 1799 Benjamin Wright of Amherst County, and great great great grandson of 1767 Francis Wright of Amherst County and 1914 William Henry Wright of Amherst County, son of 1862 Shelton H. Wright of Amherst County, grandson of 1873 Jesse Wright of Amherst County, great grandson of 1830 Moses Wright of Amherst County, great great grandson of 1799 Benjamin Wright of Amherst County, and great great great grandson of 1767 Francis Wright of Amherst County

Appendix: Amherst County, Virginia, Deed Records

Book/Page	Date	Grantor	Grantee	Instrument	Identification
PP 106	1883/11/24	William H. Wright & Emma N. Wright	Thomas L. Jones	Deed	1914 William H. Wright of Bedford County, son of 1874 Shelton Wright of Nelson County, grandson of 1850 Jesse Wright of Amherst County, great grandson of 1799 Benjamin Wright of Amherst County, and great great grandson of 1767 Francis Wright of Amherst County
PP 291	1883/12/06	Jesse E. Adams & Fannie E. Adams	Charles Wright's Heirs	Deed	Charles Wright, son of Benjamin Wright, grandson of 1830 Moses Wright of Amherst County, great grandson of 1799 Benjamin Wright of Amherst County, and great great grandson of 1767 Francis Wright of Amherst County
PP 292	1884/01/02	Dison C. Blanks & Ann E. Blanks & Samuel J. Turner & Sarah B. Turner	Charles Wright's Heirs	Deed	Charles Wright, son of Benjamin Wright, grandson of 1830 Moses Wright of Amherst County, great grandson of 1799 Benjamin Wright of Amherst County, and great great grandson of 1767 Francis Wright of Amherst County
PP 174	1884/07/05	C. L. Wright & Rosa E. Wright & Geo. W. Staples & Mary T. Staples & William J. Tucker & Ann H. Tucker & Thos. G. Tucker & Sarah P. Tucker & James E. Caldwell & Emma N. Caldwell & William R. Eggleston & Ella S. Eggleston & Jno. D. Hudson & Elizabeth Hudson & Wm. H. Wright & Mollie E. Wright	Wm. M. Thompson	Deed	1914 Cary Lucas "Luke" Wright of Lynchburg, son of 1862 Shelton H. Wright of Amherst County, grandson of 1873 Jesse Wright of Amherst County, great grandson of 1830 Moses Wright of Amherst County, great great grandson of 1799 Benjamin Wright of Amherst County, and great great great grandson of 1767 Francis Wright of Amherst County and 1914 William Henry Wright of Amherst County, son of 1862 Shelton H. Wright of Amherst County, grandson of 1873 Jesse Wright of Amherst County, great grandson of 1830 Moses Wright of Amherst County, great great grandson of 1799 Benjamin Wright of Amherst County, and great great great grandson of 1767 Francis Wright of Amherst County
QQ 149	1885/10/03	L. M. Campbell	Charles H. Wright	Deed	
RR 044	1886/11/11	Hugh Wright	Wm. G. Loving, Tr.	D T	

Appendix: Amherst County, Virginia, Deed Records

Book/Page	Date	Grantor	Grantee	Instrument	Identification
SS 597	1887/07/23	Stephen Johnson, Jr. & Jane Johnson	Mrs. Susan Wright	Deed	
SS 137	1888/05/07	Hugh Wright & E. B. McGinnes & Sallie P. McGinnes & V. McGinnis & Billie K. McGinnis & Ro. A. Coghill	B. B. Haile	Deed	
SS 260	1889/03/16	Jno. Thompson Jr's Exr	Hiram Wright & Alexander Davis	Deed	
SS 335	1889/05/28	Mrs. M. J. Wright	F. J. Harris, Tr.	D T	
SS 376	1889/07/09	P. J. Wright	John R. Williams, Tr.	D T	1903 Phillip James Wright of Richmond City, son of 1853 John Woodson Wright of Cumberland County, grandson of 1838 William Wright of Cumberland County, great grandson of 1774 George Wright of Cumberland County, and great great grandson of 1769 George Wright of Essex County
WW 193	1889/09/07	S. A. Wright	Ro. A., & W. S. Kent	Assmt	Samuel Anderson Wright, son of 1873 John Patterson Wright of Campbell County, grandson of 1811 John Wright of Campbell County, and great grandson of Robert Wright, Sr. (Campbell County)
SS 566	1890/02/01	Amanda L. Wright & Nina L. Wright	Robert A. Lancaster	Deed	Ann Amanda Wright, daughter of 1853 John Woodson Wright of Cumberland County, granddaughter of 1838 William Wright of Cumberland County, great granddaughter of 1774 George Wright of Cumberland County, and great great granddaughter of 1769 George Wright of Essex County and Nina L. Wright, daughter of 1853 John Woodson Wright of Cumberland County, granddaughter of 1838 William Wright of Cumberland County, great granddaughter of 1774 George Wright of Cumberland County, and great great granddaughter of 1769 George Wright of Essex County

0125(102207)

Appendix: Amherst County, Virginia, Deed Records

Book/Page	Date	Grantor	Grantee	Instrument	Identification
SS 564	1890/02/01	P. P. Winston, Com.	Amanda L. Wright & Nina L. Wright	Deed	Ann Amanda Wright, daughter of 1853 John Woodson Wright of Cumberland County, granddaughter of 1838 William Wright of Cumberland County, great granddaughter of 1774 George Wright of Cumberland County, and great great granddaughter of 1769 George Wright of Essex County and Nina L. Wright, daughter of 1853 John Woodson Wright of Cumberland County, granddaughter of 1838 William Wright of Cumberland County, great granddaughter of 1774 George Wright of Cumberland County, and great great granddaughter of 1769 George Wright of Essex County
TT 144	1890/05/30	Hiram Wright & Superintendent & Board of Trustees of Schools & Abner Davis & Mathew Davis & John J. Davis	Baptist Church	Deed	
TT 224	1890/10/17	J. M. Henderson	Paul C. Wright	Deed	Paul C. Wright, son of 1870 William Wright of Amherst County, grandson of 1850 Jesse Wright of Nelson County, great grandson of 1799 Benjamin Wright of Amherst County, and great great grandson of 1767 Francis Wright of Amherst County
TT 226	1890/10/18	Jno. H. Christian & Olivia Christian	William G. Wright	Deed	William G. Wright, son of 1870 William Wright of Amherst County, grandson of 1850 Jesse Wright of Nelson County, great grandson of 1799 Benjamin Wright of Amherst County, and great great grandson of 1767 Francis Wright of Amherst County
UU 056	1891/03/23	Eliza S. Pollard & Stephen Adams, Tr. & Mary F. Chalmers & Nannie R. Pannill & J. Knox Pannill, Tr.	John J. Wright	Deed	
TT 442	1891/06/29	Amherst Company	William A. Wright	Deed	

Appendix: Amherst County, Virginia, Deed Records

Book/Page	Date	Grantor	Grantee	Instrument	Identification
UU 057	1891/09/04	Jno. H. Parr, Tr.	Jno. J. Wright	Deed	
VV 052	1892/02/17	Thos. Whitehead, Jr. & Sara L. Whitehead	Sam'l H. Wright	Deed	
UU 118	1892/06/28	John R. Wright & Mary L. Wright	John W. Parrish	Deed	1928 John R. Wright of Augusta County, son of 1854 Thompson A. Wright of Rockbridge County, grandson of 1815 John Wright of Prince William County, great grandson of William Wright, great great grandson of 1765 Richard Wright of Prince William County, and probably great great great grandson of 1700 Richard Wright of Stafford County
UU 153	1892/10/06	William A. Wright & Lucy C. Wright	The Amherst Co.	Deed	
UU 167	1892/10/13	Taylor Berry, Comr.	Alice Wright	Deed	
UU 399	1893/03/09	Thomas Whitehead, Jr.	James M. Wright	Deed	
UU 325	1893/06/28	C. L. Wright & R. E. Wright & William H. Wright	C. M. Blackford, Tr.	D T	1914 Cary Lucas "Luke" Wright of Lynchburg, son of 1873 Jesse Wright of Amherst County, grandson of 1830 Moses Wright of Amherst County, great grandson of 1799 Benjamin Wright of Amherst County, and great great grandson of 1767 Francis Wright of Amherst County and 1914 William Henry Wright of Amherst County, son of 1873 Jesse Wright of Amherst County, grandson of 1830 Moses Wright of Amherst County, great grandson of 1799 Benjamin Wright of Amherst County, and great great grandson of 1767 Francis Wright of Amherst County

Appendix: Amherst County, Virginia, Deed Records

Book/Page	Date	Grantor	Grantee	Instrument	Identification
UU 353	1893/08/03	Rachel S. Wright & Nannie Wright & Paul C. Wright & Sallie C. Wright	J. W. Myers	Deed	Rachel S. (Camden) Wright, widow of 1870 William Wright of Amherst County, a son of 1850 Jesse Wright of Nelson County, grandson of 1799 Benjamin Wright of Amherst County, and great grandson of 1767 Francis Wright of Amherst County and Paul C. Wright, son of 1870 William Wright of Amherst County, grandson of 1850 Jesse Wright of Nelson County, great grandson of 1799 Benjamin Wright of Amherst County, and great great grandson of 1767 Francis Wright of Amherst County and Sarah C. "Sallie" Wright, daughter of 1870 William Wright of Amherst County, granddaughter of 1850 Jesse Wright of Nelson County, great granddaughter of 1799 Benjamin Wright of Amherst County, and great great granddaughter of 1767 Francis Wright of Amherst County and Nancy S. Wright, daughter of 1870 William Wright of Amherst County, granddaughter of 1850 Jesse Wright of Nelson County, great granddaughter of 1799 Benjamin Wright of Amherst County, and great great granddaughter of 1767 Francis Wright of Amherst County
UU 401	1893/09/13	Wm. Z. Lackland & Susan E. Lackland	James M. Wright	Deed	
UU 362	1893/09/13	J. Carter Wright	Hugh A. White, Tr.	D T	
53 489	1893/12/17	Robert A. Kent & Nannie M. Kent & Walter S. Kent & Virginia A. Kent	Samuel A. Wright	Deed	Samuel Anderson Wright, son of 1873 John Patterson Wright of Campbell County, grandson of 1811 John Wright of Campbell County, and great grandson of Robert Wright, Sr. (Campbell County)
UU 467	1893/12/22	Patrick H. Wood	Jas. W. Wright, Tr.	Deed	
VV 152	1894/09/21	Chas. H. Wright	L. Miller, Tr.	D T	1941 Charles Henry Wright of Amherst County, son of David S. Wright

Appendix: Amherst County, Virginia, Deed Records

Book/Page	Date	Grantor	Grantee	Instrument	Identification
VV 358	1894/12/05	W. Henry Wright	Board of Supervisors of Amherst	Deed	1914 William Henry Wright of Amherst County, son of 1862 Shelton H. Wright of Amherst County, grandson of 1873 Jesse Wright of Amherst County, great grandson of 1830 Moses Wright of Amherst County, great great grandson of 1799 Benjamin Wright of Amherst County, and great great great grandson of 1767 Francis Wright of Amherst County
VV 276	1894/12/12	Charles H. Wright & Mary J. Wright	Campbell & Campbell	B S	Charles H. Wright, son of 1849 Moses Wright of Nelson County, grandson of 1830 Moses Wright of Amherst County, great grandson of 1799 Benjamin Wright of Amherst County, and great great grandson of 1767 Francis Wright of Amherst County and Mary Jane (Wright) Wright, daughter of 1873 Jesse Wright of Amherst County, granddaughter of 1830 Moses Wright of Amherst County, great granddaughter of 1799 Benjamin Wright of Amherst County, and great great granddaughter of 1767 Francis Wright of Amherst County
VV 341	1895/03/16	J. M. Wright	Lynchburg Perp. Building & L. Co.	D T	
VV 362	1895/04/15	J. Phil Shaner's Adm.	E. M. Wright	Deed	
VV 451	1895/08/02	Ed. M. Wright	Sam'l P. Wingfield	Deed	
VV 438	1895/08/26	W. H. Wright & Anna R. Wright	Rosa E. Wright	Deed	Grantor: 1914 William Henry Wright of Amherst County, son of 1862 Shelton H. Wright of Amherst County, grandson of 1873 Jesse Wright of Amherst County, great grandson of 1830 Moses Wright of Amherst County, great great grandson of 1799 Benjamin Wright of Amherst County, and great great great grandson of 1767 Francis Wright of Amherst County Grantee: Rosa Emily (Cash) Wright, wife of 1914 William Henry Wright of Amherst County, a son of 1862 Shelton H. Wright of Amherst County, grandson of 1873 Jesse Wright of Amherst County, great grandson of 1830 Moses Wright of Amherst County, great great grandson of 1799 Benjamin Wright of Amherst County, and great great great grandson of 1767 Francis Wright of Amherst County

Appendix: Amherst County, Virginia, Deed Records

Book/Page	Date	Grantor	Grantee	Instrument	Identification
VV 437	1895/08/26	C. L. Wright & Rosa E. Wright	W. H. Wright	Deed	Grantor: 1914 Cary Lucas "Luke" Wright of Lynchburg, son of 1873 Jesse Wright of Amherst County, grandson of 1830 Moses Wright of Amherst County, great grandson of 1799 Benjamin Wright of Amherst County, and great great grandson of 1767 Francis Wright of Amherst County Grantee: 1914 William Henry Wright of Amherst County, son of 1873 Jesse Wright of Amherst County, grandson of 1830 Moses Wright of Amherst County, great grandson of 1799 Benjamin Wright of Amherst County, and great great grandson of 1767 Francis Wright of Amherst County
VV 458	1895/09/01	Charles H. Wright	Littleton Miller, Tr.	D T	1941 Charles Henry Wright of Amherst County, son of David S. Wright
WW 467	1895/09/05	J. W. Myers	Paul C. Wright & Nancy S. Wright & Sallie C. Wright	Deed	Paul C. Wright, son of 1870 William Wright of Amherst County, grandson of 1850 Jesse Wright of Nelson County, great grandson of 1799 Benjamin Wright of Amherst County, and great great grandson of 1767 Francis Wright of Amherst County and Sarah C. "Sallie" Wright, daughter of 1870 William Wright of Amherst County, granddaughter of 1850 Jesse Wright of Nelson County, great granddaughter of 1799 Benjamin Wright of Amherst County, and great great granddaughter of 1767 Francis Wright of Amherst County and Nancy S. Wright, daughter of 1870 William Wright of Amherst County, granddaughter of 1850 Jesse Wright of Nelson County, great granddaughter of 1799 Benjamin Wright of Amherst County, and great great granddaughter of 1767 Francis Wright of Amherst County
VV 452	1895/09/13	Helen Maria Abbott	B. W. Wright	Deed	Benjamin Walter Wright, son of 1880 Benjamin Edward Wright of Amherst County, grandson of 1881 William P. Wright of Appomattox County, great grandson of Charles Wright, and great great grandson of Robert Wright, Sr. (Campbell County)

Appendix: Amherst County, Virginia, Deed Records

Book/Page	Date	Grantor	Grantee	Instrument	Identification
VV 468	1895/09/14	B. W. Wright & Rose Wright	G. W. Mays	D T	Benjamin Walter Wright, son of 1880 Benjamin Edward Wright of Amherst County, grandson of 1881 William P. Wright of Appomattox County, great grandson of Charles Wright, and great great grandson of Robert Wright, Sr. (Campbell County)
WW 317	1896/10/16	Jno. E. Wright & Katie Wright	Lynchburg Trust & Savings Bank	Deed	
YY 036	1897/03/26	J. T. Coleman, Comr.	W. H. Wright, Tr. & Rosa E. Wright	Deed	1914 William Henry Wright of Amherst County, son of 1862 Shelton H. Wright of Amherst County, grandson of 1873 Jesse Wright of Amherst County, great grandson of 1830 Moses Wright of Amherst County, great great grandson of 1799 Benjamin Wright of Amherst County, and great great great grandson of 1767 Francis Wright of Amherst County and Rosa Emily (Cash) Wright, wife of 1914 William Henry Wright of Amherst County, a son of 1862 Shelton H. Wright of Amherst County, grandson of 1873 Jesse Wright of Amherst County, great grandson of 1830 Moses Wright of Amherst County, great great grandson of 1799 Benjamin Wright of Amherst County, and great great great grandson of 1767 Francis Wright of Amherst County
YY 268	1897/09/20	C. L. Jennings	C. W. Wright	Deed	
XX 210	1897/11/01	E. M. Wright	Lynchburg Perp. B. & L. Co.	D T	
XX 478	1898/06/08	B. W. Wright & w.	I. H. Adams, Jr.	D T	Benjamin Walter Wright, son of 1880 Benjamin Edward Wright of Amherst County, grandson of 1881 William P. Wright of Appomattox County, great grandson of Charles Wright, and great great grandson of Robert Wright, Sr. (Campbell County)
YY 136	1898/09/14	Virginia B. Wright & C. C. Wright & Mrs. M. J. Gilbert & Norvell P. Gilbert & Harry E. Gilbert	W. B. Rucker	Deed	

Appendix: Amherst County, Virginia, Deed Records

Book/Page		Date	Grantor	Grantee	Instrument	Identification
YY	300	1899/02/02	Mary T. Staples	Rosa E. Wright	Deed	Rosa Emily (Cash) Wright, wife of 1914 William Henry Wright of Amherst County, a son of 1862 Shelton H. Wright of Amherst County, grandson of 1873 Jesse Wright of Amherst County, great grandson of 1830 Moses Wright of Amherst County, great great grandson of 1799 Benjamin Wright of Amherst County, and great great great grandson of 1767 Francis Wright of Amherst County
YY	300	1899/02/14	J. E. Caldwell & Emma N. Caldwell	R. E. Wright	Deed	Rosa Emily (Cash) Wright, wife of 1914 William Henry Wright of Amherst County, a son of 1862 Shelton H. Wright of Amherst County, grandson of 1873 Jesse Wright of Amherst County, great grandson of 1830 Moses Wright of Amherst County, great great grandson of 1799 Benjamin Wright of Amherst County, and great great great grandson of 1767 Francis Wright of Amherst County
52	024	1899/06/16	Edward Drummond & Parlina Drummond	Benjamin W. Wright	Deed	Benjamin Walter Wright, son of 1880 Benjamin Edward Wright of Amherst County, grandson of 1881 William P. Wright of Appomattox County, great grandson of Charles Wright, and great great grandson of Robert Wright, Sr. (Campbell County)
ZZ	443	1899/08/05	C. L. Scott, Spl Comr.	W. A. Wright, Tr.	Deed	
YY	479	1899/09/01	P. J. Wright	Thos. D. Christian, Tr.	D T	1903 Philip James Wright of Richmond City, son of 1853 John Woodson Wright of Cumberland County, grandson of 1838 William Wright of Cumberland County, great grandson of 1774 George Wright of Cumberland County, and great great grandson of 1769 George Wright of Essex County

Appendix: Amherst County, Virginia, Deed Records

Book/Page	Date	Grantor	Grantee	Instrument	Identification
ZZ 136	1900/03/14	C. L. Wright & Rosa E. Wright & W. H. Wright	D. H. Howard, Tr.	D T	1914 William Henry Wright of Amherst County, son of 1862 Shelton H. Wright of Amherst County, grandson of 1873 Jesse Wright of Amherst County, great grandson of 1830 Moses Wright of Amherst County, great great grandson of 1799 Benjamin Wright of Amherst County, and great great great grandson of 1767 Francis Wright of Amherst County and 1914 Cary Lucas "Luke" Wright of Lynchburg, son of 1862 Shelton H. Wright of Amherst County, grandson of 1873 Jesse Wright of Amherst County, great grandson of 1830 Moses Wright of Amherst County, great great grandson of 1799 Benjamin Wright of Amherst County, and great great great grandson of 1767 Francis Wright of Amherst County
ZZ 358	1900/07/24	E. M. Wright	W. G. Cooper	Deed	
ZZ 475	1900/10/06	Samuel H. Wright & Annie L. Wright	Daniel L. Chick & Grace A. Chick	Deed	Samuel H. Wright, son of 1894 David Staples Wright of Amherst County, grandson of 1873 Robert D. Wright of Amherst County, great grandson of Charles Wright, and great great grandson of Robert Wright, Sr. (Campbell County)
51 214	1901/04/08	J. B. Phelps & Amanda E. Phelps	Nannie E. Wright	Deed	
51 394	1901/12/24	P. J. Wright	C. T. Moore	Deed	1903 Philip James Wright of Richmond City, son of 1853 John Woodson Wright of Cumberland County, grandson of 1838 William Wright of Cumberland County, great grandson of 1774 George Wright of Cumberland County, and great great grandson of 1769 George Wright of Essex County
52 023	1902/01/15	P. H. Drummond & Fannie E. Drummond	Benjamin W. Wright	Deed	Benjamin Walter Wright, son of 1880 Benjamin Edward Wright of Amherst County, grandson of 1881 William P. Wright of Appomattox County, great grandson of Charles Wright, and great great grandson of Robert Wright, Sr. (Campbell County)

Appendix: Amherst County, Virginia, Deed Records

Book/Page		Date	Grantor	Grantee	Instrument	Identification
52	025	1902/01/15	Henley Drummond	Benjamin W. Wright	Deed	Benjamin Walter Wright, son of 1880 Benjamin Edward Wright of Amherst County, grandson of 1881 William P. Wright of Appomattox County, great grandson of Charles Wright, and great great grandson of Robert Wright, Sr. (Campbell County)
52	026	1902/02/14	Benj. W. Wright & Annie E. Wright	H. S. Myers, Trustee	D T	Benjamin Walter Wright, son of 1880 Benjamin Edward Wright of Amherst County, grandson of 1881 William P. Wright of Appomattox County, great grandson of Charles Wright, and great great grandson of Robert Wright, Sr. (Campbell County)
52	091	1902/04/10	Rosa E. Wright & C. L. Wright	F. S. Kirkpatric & D. H. Howard, Tr.	D T	1914 Cary Lucas "Luke" Wright of Lynchburg, son of 1862 Shelton H. Wright of Amherst County, grandson of 1873 Jesse Wright of Amherst County, great grandson of 1830 Moses Wright of Amherst County, great great grandson of 1799 Benjamin Wright of Amherst County, and great great great grandson of 1767 Francis Wright of Amherst County
52	091	1902/04/10	C. L. Wright & Rosa E. Wright	F. E. Kirkpatrick & C. H. Howard, Trustees	D T	1914 Cary Lucas "Luke" Wright of Lynchburg, son of 1862 Shelton H. Wright of Amherst County, grandson of 1873 Jesse Wright of Amherst County, great grandson of 1830 Moses Wright of Amherst County, great great grandson of 1799 Benjamin Wright of Amherst County, and great great great grandson of 1767 Francis Wright of Amherst County
52	184	1902/06/25	E. M. Wright & Annie L. Wright	Mary Alice North & Calvin O. North	Deed	
52	184	1902/06/25	E. M. Wright & Annie L. Wright	Mary Alice North & Calvin O. North	Deed	
52	474	1902/08/20	Robt. M. Mitchell & Lucie R. Mitchell & Lillie J. Woodson & J. R. Woodson	Nannie E. Wright	Deed	

Appendix: Amherst County, Virginia, Deed Records

Book/Page		Date	Grantor	Grantee	Instrument	Identification
52	478	1902/09/20	Z. T. Cooper & Bettie S. Cooper	Samuel H. Wright	Deed	Samuel H. Wright, son of 1894 David Staples Wright of Amherst County, grandson of 1873 Robert D. Wright of Amherst County, great grandson of Charles Wright, and great great grandson of Robert Wright, Sr. (Campbell County)
53	126	1902/12/22	W. A. Wright	Kate Wright	Deed	
53	383	1903/03/21	E. L. Dameron & Mary L. Dameron	Mrs. Sarah D. Wright	Deed	
53	460	1903/08/15	P. Henson & Mary S. Henson	Hugh Wright	Deed	
53	467	1903/11/30	George A. Brook & Mary E. Brook	Annie L. Wright	Deed	
53	467	1903/11/30	George A. Brook & Mary E. Brook	E. M. Wright & Annie L. Wright	Deed	
53	490	1903/12/19	Samuel A. Wright & Elizabeth M. Wright	Lynchburg Per Bld'g & Loan Co.	D T	Samuel Anderson Wright, son of 1873 John Patterson Wright of Campbell County, grandson of 1811 John Wright of Campbell County, and great grandson of Robert Wright, Sr. (Campbell County)

INDEX

Abbott, Helen Maria, 40
Adams, Fannie E., 34
Adams, Jesse E., 34
Adams, Stephen, 36
Adams, Jr., I. H., 41
Alford, John, 6
Alfred, Susanna, 13
Alfred, Thomas, 13
Armistead, William, 13
Berry, Martha J., 31
Berry, Marvel L., 16
Berry, Taylor, 31, 37
Bibb, William, 6
Bibb, Wm., 6
Bird, Henry W., 21
Blackford, C. M., 37
Blanks, Ann E., 34
Blanks, Dison C., 26, 34
Bonds, John, 15
Bonds, William, 15
Bowling, James, 9
Bowling, Lettie, 9
Brockman, Samuel W., 33
Brockman, Susan, 33
Brook, George A., 45
Brook, Mary E., 45
Brown, Benjamin, 28, 33
Brown, James, 2
Brown, Robert M., 28, 33
Brown, S., 28
Brown, S. A., 33
Brown, Sally P., 28, 33
Bryant, Parmenos, 9
Bryant, Parmenus, 8
Burt, Wm., 2
Burton, James H., 8

Burton, James Halley, 3
Caldwell, Emma N., 34, 42
Caldwell, J. E., 42
Caldwell, James E., 34
Camden, John, 10, 12
Camden, John F., 18, 20, 22, 24, 25
Camden, John S., 20, 21
Camden, Sally, 22
Camden, W. G., 23
Campbell, Charles A., 25
Campbell, Elizabeth, 19
Campbell, Frances, 13
Campbell, George, 13
Campbell, James, 17, 18
Campbell, John, 4, 8, 10, 13, 14
Campbell, L. M., 34
Campbell, Lucy, 13
Campbell, Nancy, 25
Campbell, Shannon D., 19
Campbell, Wiatt, 18, 19
Campbell, William, 13
Campbell, Wyatt, 16
Carrington, George, 1
Carter, Abraham, 6, 9
Carter, Edward, 5, 9
Carter, Maryann, 2
Carter, Peter, 2
Cartwright, John, 8
Cash, Cary I., 28
Cash, Howard, 9
Cash, John, 22
Cash, Martha, 28
Chalmers, Mary F., 36
Chick, Daniel L., 43
Chick, Grace A., 43
Childress, Polly, 13

Christian, Amelius, 28, 32
Christian, Camillus, 27
Christian, Jno. H., 36
Christian, John H., 27, 30
Christian, Mary D., 26
Christian, Olivia, 36
Christian, Sam'l W., 13
Christian, Samuel B., 26
Christian, Thos. D., 42
Cochnower, Geo. F., 31
Cocke, James, 6
Coghill, Ro. A., 35
Coleman, J. T., 41
Cooper, Bettie S., 45
Cooper, W. G., 43
Cooper, Z. T., 45
Coppedge, James W., 14
Crawford, John, 6
Crawford, Nelson, 7
Crutcher, Robt. Ab., 13
Dameron, E. L., 45
Dameron, Mary L., 45
Davidson, S. S., 31
Davis, Abner, 36
Davis, Alexander, 35
Davis, Charles C., 27
Davis, Henrietta C. C., 27
Davis, Mathew, 36
Dawson, Martin, 3
Dillard, Jo., 12
Dillard, John, 16
Dillard, Joseph, 11, 13
Dillard, Judith, 13
Dillard Jr., W., 30
Drummond, Edward, 42
Drummond, Fannie E., 43

Drummond, Henley, 44
Drummond, P. H., 43
Drummond, Parlina, 42
Eastains, John, 2
Edmonds, Samuel, 5, 7
Edmunds, Alice, 7
Edwards, Elloner, 4
Edwards, Jos., 4
Edwards, Joseph, 4
Eggleston, Ella S., 32, 34
Eggleston, William, 32
Eggleston, William R., 34
Ellis, Richard T., 11
Evans, Nancy, 15
Evans, William, 19
Farrar, John, 11, 12
Farrar, Mary, 11, 12
Fletcher, Elijah, 22
Fletcher, Sidney, 25
Fulcher, Geo., 24, 29
Garland, David S., 9, 14
Garland, Jane H., 14
Garland, Samuel M., 22
Gatewood, Cathorine, 4
Gatewood, Larkin, 4
Gilbert, Harry E., 41
Gilbert, John C., 13
Gilbert, M. J., 41
Gillaspie, Alexander, 9
Gillaspie, George, 9
Gillaspie, Lewis, 9
Gillenwaters, Elisha, 11
Gilliam, Deverix, 2
Gilliam, Edith, 2
Gilliam, Jr., Archelaus, 20
Gooch, Philip, 7

Goode, Daniel, 21
Goodrich, Thomas, 7
Goodwin, John Henry, 3
Goodwin, Marbell E., 23
Goolsby, Jno., 18
Gosney, Henry, 5
Grymes, Mary, 1
Grymes, Philip, 1
Haile, B. B., 35
Harris, F. J., 35
Harris, William, 1, 2
Harris, William Lee, 6
Harrison, Richard, 4
Healey, J. W., 31
Henderson, J. M., 36
Henson, Mary S., 45
Henson, P., 45
Hibit, William, 1
Higginbotham, Daniel, 8
Higginbotham, James, 19
Higginbotham, John, 9
Hill, Nathaniel, 5
Hill, Thomas G., 22
Hollandsworth, Wm., 3
Houchin, William, 6
Howard, C. H., 44
Howard, D. H., 43, 44
Hudson, Elizabeth W., 32
Hudson, Jno. D., 32, 34
Isbell, Angelina T., 30
Isbell, Robert, 30
Jackson, William, 15
Jennings, C. L., 41
Johnson, Jane, 35
Johnson, John, 2, 4
Johnson, Jr., Stephen, 35
Johnston, Dicey, 3
Johnston, John, 3
Jones, Betsy, 9

Jones, Hezekiah, 19
Jones, Thomas L., 34
Keith, Peyton, 15
Kelley, William, 14
Kelley, Wm., 14
Kelly, William, 11, 12
Kennedy, Betsey, 12
Kennedy, Betsy, 11, 12
Kennedy, Druzilly, 11
Kennedy, Jesse, 11, 12
Kennedy, Joseph, 11, 12
Kent, Nannie M., 38
Kent, Ro. A., 35
Kent, Robert A., 38
Kent, Virginia A., 38
Kent, W. S., 35
Kent, Walter S., 38
Kirkpatric, F. S., 44
Kirkpatrick, F. E., 44
Lackland, Susan E., 38
Lackland, Wm. Z., 38
Lancaster, Robert A., 35
Landrum, Patsey, 7
Landrum, Young, 7
Lilly, William, 7
Lomax, Lunsford, 1
London, Jno, 12
London, John, 11
Lovell, Elizabeth, 2
Lovell, Geo., 2
Loving, John, 2, 5
Loving, Joseph, 7
Loving, Wm. G., 33, 34
Mantiply, Nathaniel, 3
Martin, Hudson, 4
Martin, James S., 14
Martin, William, 4
Massie, Jno., 15
Massie Sr., John, 15

Mays, Bransford, 20
Mays, Charles, 20
Mays, G. W., 41
McAlexander, Alexander, 8
McAlister, William C., 15
McAllister, Wm. G., 16
McGinnes, E. B., 35
McGinnes, Sallie P., 35
McGinnis, Billie K., 35
McGinnis, Mary V., 25
McGinnis, Valerius, 25
Mead, Prudence Watkins, 13
Mead, Stith, 13
Melton, John, 8
Miller, John, 4
Miller, L., 38
Miller, Littleton, 40
Miller, M. H., 33
Mitchell, Charles L., 21
Mitchell, Jno., 21
Mitchell, Lucie R., 44
Mitchell, Robt. M., 44
Moore, C. T., 43
Morrill, William, 3
Murphy, James, 7, 8
Myers, H. S., 44
Myers, J. W., 38, 40
North, Calvin O., 44
North, Mary Alice, 44
Nunnelley, Daniel A., 21
Pannill, J. Knox, 36
Parr, Jno. H., 37
Parrish, John W., 37
Patterson, Caroline T., 33
Patterson, James M., 33
Patteson, Caroline T., 28
Patteson, James M., 28
Payton, Mary, 4
Payton, Valentine, 4

Payton, Vaulintine, 4
Pendleton, Annie S., 27
Pendleton, R. A., 29
Pendleton, Ro. A., 30
Pendleton, Robert A., 27
Penn, Gabriel, 2
Penn, Lucy M., 33
Penn, Maria, 33
Penn, Thomas, 10
Phelps, Amanda E., 43
Phelps, J. B., 43
Philips, Moses, 15
Plunkett, Willis H., 16
Poindexter, Drusilla, 12
Poindexter, John, 12
Pollard, Eliza S., 36
Pollard, Elizabeth, 10
Pollard, Elizabeth B., 8
Pollard, Richard C., 8, 10
Porter, Joseph, 30
Pryor, William, 7, 10
Richeson, Jesse, 17
Richeson, John, 10
Richeson, Thomas, 20
Right, Levicey W., 18
Right, Rhoda W., 18
Robinson, John, 1
Rowsa, John, 2
Rowsa, Mary, 2
Rucker, W. B., 41
Scott, C. L., 42
Shaner, J. Phil, 39
Shelton, Joseph, 5, 8
Smith, Genova, 22
Smith, Henry E., 30
Smith, Jacob, 22
Smoot, Lucy F., 25
Smoot, Susanna, 12
Smoot(?), Susanna, 11

Staples, Geo. W., 34
Staples, Mary T., 34, 42
Teas, Thompson, 5
Teneson, John, 3
Terry, William P., 30
Thompson, Lucy, 25
Thompson, Wm. M., 34
Thompson Jr., Jno., 35
Thurmond, Judith, 6
Thurmond, Philip, 6
Tinsely, Martin D., 22
Tinsley, Robert, 22
Tucker, Ann H., 34
Tucker, Ann J. (Wright), 31
Tucker, Ellen, 26
Tucker, Nancy J., 14
Tucker, Sarah P., 34
Tucker, Sarah P. (Wright), 31
Tucker, Thos. G., 31, 34
Tucker, William J., 34
Tucker, Wyatt, 26
Tuggle, John, 2
Turner, Samuel J., 34
Turner, Sarah B., 34
Waller, William M., 21
Ward, John, 4
Ware, William, 7, 9, 10, 11
Watson, Edwin, 29
Watts, Elizabeth B., 23
Watts, Gustavious A., 23
Wedderbourn, Wm., 6
Welch, John, 1
White, Hugh A., 38
Whitehead, Sara L., 37
Whitehead, Jr., Thomas, 37
Whitehead, Jr., Thos., 37
Whittle, Oney, 12
Wilcher, Wm. P., 25
Williams, John R., 35

Wilsher, Thomas, 1
Wilsher, William P., 24
Wilsher, Wm. P., 25
Wingfield, Sam'l P., 39
Winston, P. P., 36
Wittle, Oney, 11
Wood, Patrick H., 38
Woodroof, John, 1
Woodson, David S., 24, 27, 29
Woodson, Lillie J., 44
Wright, Alice, 1
Wright, Alice, 37
Wright, Amanda L., 35, 36
Wright, Ambrose F., 15, 16
Wright, Andrew, 3
Wright, Anna R., 39
Wright, Annie E., 44
Wright, Annie L., 43, 44, 45
Wright, Archilles, 7
Wright, Augustine, 1
Wright, B. E., 30
Wright, B. W., 40, 41
Wright, Benj. W., 44
Wright, Benjamin, 2, 5, 6, 10, 16, 19
Wright, Benjamin W., 42, 43, 44
Wright, Burch W., 30
Wright, C. C., 41
Wright, C. L., 28, 29, 31, 32, 33, 34, 37, 40, 43, 44
Wright, C. W., 41
Wright, Cary L., 26, 30
Wright, Charles, 17, 22, 26, 34
Wright, Charles H., 33, 34, 39, 40
Wright, Chas. H., 29, 31, 33, 38
Wright, Cordelia, 3, 4
Wright, Cordelo or Dillie, 4
Wright, Cynthia, 11, 12
Wright, Daniel L., 26
Wright, Jr., Daniel Lewis, 30

Wright, Dicey, 9, 16, 26
Wright, Dillie or Cordelo, 4
Wright, E. M., 39, 41, 43, 44, 45
Wright, Ed. M., 39
Wright, Eliza, 17, 19
Wright, Eliza A., 21
Wright, Elizabeth, 1, 2, 3, 4, 5, 8, 13, 17, 22, 25
Wright, Elizabeth M., 45
Wright, Ellen, 30
Wright, Ellen Jane, 17, 19
Wright, Ellis, 14, 15, 19
Wright, Ellis, 20, 21, 24
Wright, Emma N., 34
Wright, Esther, 1, 3, 8
Wright, Fielding H., 30
Wright, Geo. G., 15
Wright, George, 17, 19, 24
Wright, George G., 14, 15, 16
Wright, George W., 18
Wright, Harrison, 14
Wright, Henry, 13, 15
Wright, Henry T., 22, 25
Wright, Hiram, 35, 36
Wright, Hugh, 29, 34, 35, 45
Wright, Isaac, 1, 2, 3, 4, 5, 6, 7, 9, 10, 11
Wright, J. Carter, 38
Wright, J. M., 39
Wright, Jacob, 1, 2
Wright, James, 1, 5, 17, 19, 21
Wright, James M., 37, 38
Wright, Jas. W., 38
Wright, Jesse, 5, 6, 9, 10, 12, 13, 17, 18, 22, 25
Wright, Jr., Jesse, 8, 13, 25
Wright, Sr., Jesse, 7
Wright, Jno. E., 41
Wright, Jno. J., 37

Wright, Jno. W., 28, 32
Wright, John, 1, 2, 3, 5, 6, 8, 9, 10, 16
Wright, John C., 13
Wright, John F., 16
Wright, John J., 36
Wright, John R., 37
Wright, John W., 27, 28, 30, 33
Wright, Jordan, 8
Wright, Joseph, 14
Wright, Jourdan, 9
Wright, Kate, 45
Wright, Katie, 41
Wright, Keziah, 5, 6
Wright, Keziah (Gillenwaters), 11
Wright, Killis, 1, 3
Wright, Levicey, 17
Wright, Levicy, 19
Wright, Lewis, 14, 22
Wright, Lindsey, 8
Wright, Lucy C., 37
Wright, M. H., 28
Wright, M. J., 35
Wright, Margaret, 8
Wright, Martha C., 27
Wright, Martha H., 26, 28
Wright, Mary J., 33, 39
Wright, Mary L., 37
Wright, Mary P., 21
Wright, Melonder, 23
Wright, Menos, 1, 5, 7, 8
Wright, Mollie E., 34
Wright, Moses, 3, 4, 5, 8, 10, 13, 17, 19
Wright, Nancy, 7
Wright, Nancy S., 40
Wright, Nannie, 38
Wright, Nannie E., 43, 44
Wright, Nina L., 35, 36
Wright, P. J., 35, 42, 43
Wright, Paul, 24

Wright, Paul C., 21, 22, 24, 27, 29, 36, 38, 40
Wright, Permelia, 14
Wright, Philip J., 27, 28, 32
Wright, Phillip J., 27
Wright, R. E., 37, 42
Wright, Rachel S., 20, 23, 27, 29, 38
Wright, Rebecca, 15
Wright, Rhoda, 18, 19
Wright, Right, 21
Wright, Robert, 1, 2, 3, 4, 5, 6, 8, 11
Wright, Robert A., 31
Wright, Rosa E., 29, 30, 34, 39, 40, 41, 42, 43, 44
Wright, Rose, 41
Wright, S. A., 35
Wright, Sallie C., 38, 40
Wright, Sally, 17
Wright, Sam'l H., 37
Wright, Samuel A., 38, 45
Wright, Samuel H., 43, 45
Wright, Sara C., 27
Wright, Sarah, 3, 26
Wright, Sarah Ann (Gilliam), 20
Wright, Sarah D., 45
Wright, Shelton, 14, 15, 2324
Wright, Shelton H., 23, 24, 25
Wright, Susan, 35
Wright, Susanna, 6, 8, 9, 10
Wright, Susannah, 5, 6, 7
Wright, Syntha, 12
Wright, Thomas, 1, 2, 3, 4, 13, 14, 17, 20, 21
Wright, Virginia B., 41
Wright, W. A., 42, 45
Wright, W. H., 31, 32, 39, 40, 41, 43
Wright, W. Henry, 33, 39
Wright, Wiatt, 17, 19

Wright, William, 1, 3, 4, 8, 11, 12, 13, 14, 15, 16, 18, 19, 20, 21, 22, 23, 24, 25
Wright, Jr., William, 3
Wright Sr., William, 3
Wright, William A., 36, 37
Wright, William G., 27, 29, 36
Wright, William H., 34, 37
Wright, Wm., 1, 4
Wright, Sr., Wm., 5
Wright, Wm. H., 34
Young, John W., 14

WRIGHT FAMILY

CHANCERY COURT FILES

1804-1900

AMHERST COUNTY, VIRGINIA

Revised as of July 28, 2007

© 2007, Robert N. Grant
1916(072807)

Introduction To Appendix: Chancery Court Files for Amherst County, Virginia

This document is an appendix to a larger work titled <u>Sorting Some Of The Wrights Of Southern Virginia</u>. The work is divided into parts for each family of Wrights that has been researched. Each part is divided into two sections; the first section is text discussing the family and the evidence supporting the relationships and the second section is a descendants chart summarizing the relationships and information known about each individual.

The appendices to the work (of which this document is one) present source records for persons named Wright by county and by type of record with the identification of the person named and their Wright ancestors to the extent known.

The source for the records listed in this appendix are the following:

1) Chancery Court Files, available from the Clerk of the Circuit Court, 100 E Street, P.O. Box 462, Amherst County, Virginia 24521.

The identification of a person or their ancestor by year and county indicates their year of death and county of residence at death. For example, "1763 Thomas Wright of Bedford County" indicates that this was the Thomas Wright who died in 1763 in Bedford County. If no state is listed after the county, the state is Virginia; counties in states other than Virginia will have a state listed after the county, as in "1876 William S. Wright of Highland County, Ohio".

A parenthetical after the name indicates an identification of the person when a place of death is not yet known, as in "John Wright (Goochland County Carpenter)". A county in parentheses after the name indicates the county with which that person was most identified when no evidence of the place of death has yet been found, as in "Grief Wright (Bedford County)".

All or portions of the text and descendants charts for each Wright family identified are available from the author:

Robert N. Grant
15 Campo Bello Court   (H) 650-854-0895
Menlo Park, California 94025   (O) 650-614-3800

This is a work in progress and I would be most interested in receiving additional information about any of the persons identified in these records in order to correct any errors or expand on the information given.

1916(072807)

Appendix: Amherst County, Virginia, Chancery Court Files

Approximate Beginning Date	File	Plaintiff	Defendant	Identification
c. 1804/06/30	0000	Moses Mays	Lavinia Wright, as administrator of estate of Jordan Wright, & Lavender London	Lavinia (____) Wright, widow of 1804 Jordan Wright of Amherst County, a son of Parmenos Wright
1819/10/13	0007	Joseph Dillard	William Wright & other Kennedy heirs	1851 William Wright of Amherst County, probably son of William Wright, Jr., and grandson of William Wright (Amherst County)
1822/09/19	0000	Abram Carter	John E. Wright	John E. Wright, son of 1807 Isaac Wright of Amherst County and grandson of 1767 Francis Wright of Amherst County
1832/04/06	0001	Richard S. Ellis, Guardian	John E. Wright	John E. Wright, son of 1807 Isaac Wright of Amherst County and grandson of 1767 Francis Wright of Amherst County
1838/02/20	0014	John B. Fortune & Christopher T. Estes	Benjamin Wright, Dicey Wright, Wiatt Campbell, William Wright, Ellis Wright, Daniel Wright, George G. Wright	Benjamin Wright, son of 1830 Moses Wright of Amherst County, grandson of 1799 Benjamin Wright of Amherst County, and great grandson of 1767 Francis Wright of Amherst County, and George G. Wright, 1880 Ellis Wright of Amherst County, 1874 Shelton Wright of Nelson County, 1870 William Wright of Amherst County, and 1882 Daniel L. Wright of Amherst County, all sons of 1850 Jesse Wright of Amherst County, grandsons of 1799 Benjamin Wright of Amherst County, and great grandsons of 1767 Francis Wright of Amherst County
1839/01/23	0013	Elisha B. Estes	Ellis Wright & Daniel L. Wright	1880 Ellis Wright of Amherst County, son of 1850 Jesse Wright of Amherst County, grandson of 1799 Benjamin Wright of Amherst County, and great grandson of 1767 Francis Wright of Amherst County, and 1882 Daniel L. Wright of Amherst County, son of 1850 Jesse Wright of Amherst County, grandson of 1799 Benjamin Wright of Amherst County, and great grandson of 1767 Francis Wright of Amherst County
1842/11/14	0000	V. McGinnis	Daniel L. Wright & John F. Camden	1882 Daniel L. Wright of Amherst County, son of 1850 Jesse Wright of Amherst County, grandson of 1799 Benjamin Wright of Amherst County, and great grandson of 1767 Francis Wright of Amherst County
1844/11/07	0000	Robert D. Wright	Alexander S. Henry	1873 Robert D. Wright of Amherst County, son of Charles Wright and grandson of Robert Wright, Sr. (Campbell County)

1916(072807)

Appendix: Amherst County, Virginia, Chancery Court Files

Approximate Beginning Date	File	Plaintiff	Defendant	Identification
c. 1846/10/26	0000	E. & D. L. Wright	George H. Campbell	1880 Ellis Wright of Amherst County, son of 1850 Jesse Wright of Amherst County, grandson of 1799 Benjamin Wright of Amherst County, and great grandson of 1767 Francis Wright of Amherst County, and 1882 Daniel L. Wright of Amherst County, son of 1850 Jesse Wright of Amherst County, grandson of 1799 Benjamin Wright of Amherst County, and great grandson of 1767 Francis Wright of Amherst County
c. 1847/03/18	0000	Adelaide Pendleton	Shelton H. Wright	1862 Shelton H. Wright of Amherst County, son of 1873 Jesse Wright of Amherst County, grandson of 1830 Moses Wright of Amherst County, great grandson of 1799 Benjamin Wright of Amherst County, and great great grandson of 1767 Francis Wright of Amherst County
c. 1851/06/20	0032	Fielding H. Wright	Edward J. Davis	Fielding Hobson Wright; son of 1873 Robert D. Wright of Amherst County, grandson of Charles Wright, and great grandson of Robert Wright, Sr. (Campbell County)
c. 1852/03/00	0049	William A. Wright	George M. Purvis and other heirs of William Wright	Family of 1851 William Wright of Amherst County, probably son of William Wright, Jr., and grandson of William Wright (Amherst County)
1866/12/00	0070	Andrew J. Wright & Mary J. Wright	Heirs of Joseph Goode	1869 Andrew Jackson Wright of Amherst County, son of 1873 Jesse Wright of Amherst County, grandson of 1830 Moses Wright of Amherst County, great grandson of 1799 Benjamin Wright of Amherst County, and great great grandson of 1767 Francis Wright of Amherst County
1870/08/08	0051	Cyrus T. Bourne	Daniel L. Wright	1882 Daniel L. Wright of Amherst County, son of 1850 Jesse Wright of Amherst County, grandson of 1799 Benjamin Wright of Amherst County, and great grandson of 1767 Francis Wright of Amherst County
1877/04/00	0062B	Henry T. Wright	John R. Cunningham	
1881/08/13	0062C	Powhatan Wingfield, John E. Wingfield, James R. Wingfield, James G. White, Martha R. (Wingfield) White	Robert A. Wright & James W. Henley & S. S. Davidson	

1916(072807)

Appendix: Amherst County, Virginia, Chancery Court Files

Approximate Beginning Date	File	Plaintiff	Defendant	Identification
c. 1882/02/02	0062A	C. H. Wright, Mary J. Wright, Martha A. Campbell, Elizabeth Mays, Maurice Wright, Eady B. Campbell	Heirs of Jesse Wright	Family of 1873 Jesse Wright of Amherst County, son of 1830 Moses Wright of Amherst County, grandson of 1799 Benjamin Wright of Amherst County, and great grandson of 1767 Francis Wright of Amherst County
c. 1882/02/13	0063	Cary L. Wright & William H. Wright	Heirs of Maria W. Penn & Edward A. Penn	1914 William Henry Wright of Amherst County, son of 1862 Shelton H. Wright of Amherst County, grandson of 1873 Jesse Wright of Amherst County, great grandson of 1830 Moses Wright of Amherst County, great great grandson of 1799 Benjamin Wright of Amherst County, and great great great grandson of 1767 Francis Wright of Amherst County, and 1914 Cary Lucas "Luke" Wright of Lynchburg, son of 1862 Shelton H. Wright of Amherst County, grandson of 1873 Jesse Wright of Amherst County, great grandson of 1830 Moses Wright of Amherst County, great great grandson of 1799 Benjamin Wright of Amherst County, and great great great grandson of 1767 Francis Wright of Amherst County
c. 1889/01/07	0071	Fielding H. Wright	Heirs of Robert D. Wright	Family of 1873 Robert D. Wright of Amherst County, son of Charles Wright and grandson of Robert Wright, Sr. (Campbell County)
c. 1891/07/20	0076	S. A. Wright	A. L. Mays	Samuel Anderson Wright, son of 1873 John Patterson Wright of Campbell County, grandson of 1811 John Wright of Campbell, and great grandson of Robert Wright, Sr. (Campbell County)

INDEX

Bourne, Cyrus T., 2
Camden, John F., 1
Campbell, Eady B., 3
Campbell, George H., 2
Campbell, Martha A., 3
Campbell, Wiatt, 1
Carter, Abram, 1
Cunningham, John R., 2
Davidson, S. S., 2
Davis, Edward J., 2
Dillard, Joseph, 1
Ellis, Richard S., 1
Estes, Christopher T., 1
Estes, Elisha B., 1
Fortune, John B., 1
Goode, Joseph, 2
Henley, James W., 2
Henry, Alexander S., 1
London, Lavender, 1
Mays, A. L., 3
Mays, Elizabeth, 3
Mays, Moses, 1
McGinnis, V., 1
Pendleton, Adelaide, 2
Penn, Edward A., 3
Penn, Maria W., 3
Purvis, George M., 2
White, James G., 2
White, Martha R. (Wingfield), 2
Wingfield, James R., 2
Wingfield, John E., 2
Wingfield, Powhatan, 2
Wright, Andrew J., 2
Wright, Benjamin, 1
Wright, C. H., 3
Wright, Cary L., 3
Wright, D. L., 2

Wright, Daniel, 1
Wright, Daniel L., 1, 2
Wright, Dicey, 1
Wright, E., 2
Wright, Ellis, 1
Wright, Fielding H., 2, 3
Wright, George G., 1
Wright, Henry T., 2
Wright, Jesse, 3
Wright, John E., 1
Wright, Jordan, 1
Wright, Lavinia, 1
Wright, Mary J., 2, 3
Wright, Maurice, 3
Wright, Robert A., 2
Wright, Robert D., 1, 3
Wright, S. A., 3
Wright, Shelton H., 2
Wright, William, 1, 2
Wright, William A., 2
Wright, William H., 3

WRIGHT FAMILY

DEATH RECORDS

1853-1920

AMHERST COUNTY, VIRGINIA

Revised as of March 18, 2007

© 2007, Robert N. Grant
0413(031807)

Introduction To Appendix: Death Records for Amherst County, Virginia

This document is an appendix to a larger work titled Sorting Some Of The Wrights Of Southern Virginia. The work is divided into parts for each family of Wrights that has been researched. Each part is divided into two sections; the first section is text discussing the family and the evidence supporting the relationships and the second section is a descendants chart summarizing the relationships and information known about each individual.

The appendices to the work (of which this document is one) present source records for persons named Wright by county and by type of record with the identification of the person named and their Wright ancestors to the extent known.

The source for the records listed in this appendix is the following:

1) Amherst County, Virginia, Death Records, available from the Commonwealth of Virginia, Department of Health, Division of Vital Records, P.O. Box 1000, Richmond, Virginia 23208-1000.

The identification of a person or their ancestor by year and county indicates their year of death and county of residence at death. For example, "1763 Thomas Wright of Bedford County" indicates that this was the Thomas Wright who died in 1763 in Bedford County. If no state is listed after the county, the state is Virginia; counties in states other than Virginia will have a state listed after the county, as in "1876 William S. Wright of Highland County, Ohio".

A parenthetical after the name indicates an identification of the person when a place of death is not yet known, as in "John Wright (Goochland County Carpenter)". A county in parentheses after the name indicates the county with which that person was most identified when no evidence of the place of death has yet been found, as in "Grief Wright (Bedford County)".

All or portions of the text and descendants charts for each Wright family identified are available from the author:

Robert N. Grant
15 Campo Bello Court   (H) 650-854-0895
Menlo Park, California 94025   (O) 650-614-3800

This is a work in progress and I would be most interested in receiving additional information about any of the persons identified in these records in order to correct any errors or expand on the information given.

Appendix: Amherst County, Virginia, Death Records

Book/Page	Date	Decedent	Information	Identification
	1857/03/12	Geo. W. Wright	Place: Amherst County, Virginia Race: White Sex: Male Age: 19 Years & 11 Months Place: Amherst County, Virginia Cause: Typhoid Fever Parents: Geo. W. Wright Birthplace: Amherst Informant: Father	1857 George W. Wright of Amherst County, son of George W. Wright
	1858/00/00	____ Wright	Place: Amherst County, Virginia Race: White Sex: Female Age: 1 Month Place: Amherst Parents: Geo. & Martha Wright Birthplace: Amherst Informant: T. W. Jones	
	1858/01/00	Martha Wright	Place: Amherst County, Virginia Race: White Sex: Female Age: 21 Place: Amherst County, Virginia Cause: Consumption Parents: Mason Birthplace: Amherst Consort of: Geo. Wright Informant: T. W. Jones	Possibly Margaret A. (Mason) Wright, wife of Robert Doss Wright, a son of 1873 Robert D. Wright of Amherst County, grandson of Charles Wright, and great grandson of Robert Wright, Sr. (Campbell County)

Appendix: Amherst County, Virginia, Death Records

Book/Page	Date	Decedent	Information	Identification
	1858/06/07	Julia A. Wright	Place: Amherst County, Virginia Race: White Sex: Female Age: 50 Place: Amherst County, Virginia Cause: Consumption Parents: Jordan & E. Mays Birthplace: Wilson Consort of: A. J. Wright Informant: Husband	Julia A. (Mays) Wright, wife of A. Jackson Wright, a son of 1873 Jesse Wright of Amherst County, grandson of 1830 Moses Wright of Amherst County, great grandson of 1799 Benjamin Wright of Amherst County, and great great grandson of 1767 Francis Wright of Amherst County
	1859/00/00	Susan Wright	Place: Amherst County, Virginia Race: White Sex: Female Age: 96 Place: Amherst County, Virginia Cause: Old Age Parents: (Not Stated) Bibb Birthplace: Amherst County, Virginia Informant: Jas S. Mays	Susannah (Bibb) Wright, widow of John Wright, a son of 1776 Augustine Wright of Amherst County
	1860/08/00	____ Wright	Place: Amherst County, Virginia Race: White Sex: Male Age: 4 Years Place: Amherst Parents: Lewis & Nan Wright Birthplace: Amherst Informant: Father	Son of Daniel Lewis Wright, grandson of Benjamin Wright, great grandson of 1830 Moses Wright of Amherst County, great great grandson of 1799 Benjamin Wright of Amherst County, and great great great grandson of 1767 Francis Wright of Amherst County

Appendix: Amherst County, Virginia, Death Records

Book/Page	Date	Decedent	Information	Identification
	1864/07/00	Mary Wright	Place: Amherst County, Virginia Race: Colored Sex: Female Age: 5 Years Place: Amherst Cause: Whooping Cough Parents: Jane Wright Birthplace: Amherst	
	1865/01/00	Francis Jane Wright	Place: Amherst County, Virginia Race: White Sex: Female Age: 19 Place: Amherst Cause: (Suddenly) Parents: Shelton H. & E. Wright Birthplace: Amherst Consort of: Unmarried	Frances Jane Wright, daughter of 1862 Shelton H. Wright of Amherst County, granddaughter of 1873 Jesse Wright of Amherst County, great granddaughter of 1830 Moses Wright of Amherst County, great great granddaughter of 1799 Benjamin Wright of Amherst County, and great great great granddaughter of 1767 Francis Wright of Amherst County
	1865/06/00	____ Wright	Place: Amherst County, Virginia Race: White Sex: Male Age: 3 Days Place: Amherst Parents: D. L. & Nancy Wright Birthplace: Amherst Informant: D. Lewis Wright Relationship: Father	Son of Daniel Lewis Wright, grandson of Benjamin Wright, great grandson of 1830 Moses Wright of Amherst County, great great grandson of 1799 Benjamin Wright of Amherst County, and great great great grandson of 1767 Francis Wright of Amherst County

Appendix: Amherst County, Virginia, Death Records

Book/Page	Date	Decedent	Information	Identification
	1866/05/25	Chas H. Wright	Place: Amherst County, Virginia Race: Colored Sex: Male Age: 6 Months Place: Amherst Parents: Chas. & Susan Wright Birthplace: Amherst Informant: John Wright Relationship: Father	
	1869/07/09	Sarah Wright	Place: Amherst County, Virginia Race: White Sex: Female Age: 1 Year & 8 Months Place: Amherst Cause: Fever Parents: Wm. G. Wright & (Not Stated) Birthplace: Amherst Informant: Father	
	1869/10/01	Rowland Wright	Place: Amherst County, Virginia Race: White Sex: Male Age: 3 Years Place: Amherst Cause: Pneumonia Parents: Hugh Wright & (Not Stated) Birthplace: Amherst Informant: Father	

Appendix: Amherst County, Virginia, Death Records

Book/Page	Date	Decedent	Information	Identification
	1869/12/10	____ Wright	Place: Amherst County, Virginia Race: White Sex: Male Age: 2 Months Date of Death: December 10, 1869 Place: Amherst County, Virginia Parents: Danl. Wright Birthplace: Amherst Informant: Father	
	1870/02/17	Wm. Wright	Place: Amherst County, Virginia Race: White Sex: Male Age: 63 Place: Piney River Cause: Pneumonia Parents: J. & D. Wright Birthplace: Amherst Occupation: Farmer Informant: Wm P. Wright Relationship: Son Commissioner of the Revenue: E. S. Ware Date Record Filed: Between 1870 & 1896	1870 William Wright of Amherst County, son of 1850 Jesse Wright of Nelson County, grandson of 1799 Benjamin Wright of Amherst County, and great grandson of 1767 Francis Wright of Amherst County
	1871/07/13	Bettie A. Wright	Place: Amherst County, Virginia Race: White Sex: Female Age: 26 Date of Death: July 13, 1871 Place: Amherst Cause: Child Bed Fever Parents: Pike & Eliza Angus Birthplace: Amherst Consort of: M. W. Wright Informant: Viny Wright Relationship: Sister	

Appendix: Amherst County, Virginia, Death Records

Book/Page	Date	Decedent	Information	Identification
	1873/05/15	Jesse Wright	Place: Amherst County, Virginia Race: White Sex: Male Age: 80 Place: Amherst County Cause: Bronchitis Parents: Moses & Elizabeth Wright Birthplace: Amherst County Occupation: Farmer Consort of: Elizabeth Wright Informant: Elizabeth Wright Relationship: Wife	1873 Jesse Wright of Amherst County, son of 1830 Moses Wright of Amherst County, grandson of 1799 Benjamin Wright of Amherst County, and great grandson of 1767 Francis Wright of Amherst County
	1874/12/00	Susan Wright	Place: Amherst County, Virginia Race: Colored Sex: Female Age: 39 Place: Temperance Township Cause: Cold Parents: Henry & Winny Rose Birthplace: Amherst Occupation: Farmer Consort of: John Wright Informant: D. S. Wright Relationship: Friend	
	1875/10/24	Wm Wright	Place: Amherst County, Virginia Race: White Sex: Male Age: 20 Place: Amherst Cause: Fever Parents: James & E. A. Wright Birthplace: Lexington Informant: James H. Massey Relationship: Uncle	

Appendix: Amherst County, Virginia, Death Records

Book/Page	Date	Decedent	Information	Identification
	1876/06/14	Clarence B. Wright	Place: Amherst County, Virginia Race: White Sex: Male Age: 1 Year & 2 Months Date of Death: June 14, 1876 Place: Amherst Cause: Flux Parents: John & Emma Wright Birthplace: Amherst Informant: John Wright Relationship: Father	
	1879/05/17	Caroline Wright	Place: Amherst County, Virginia Race: Colored Sex: Female Age: 65 Date of Death: May 17, 1879 Place: Amherst County, Virginia Cause: Dropsy Parents: Charlotte Pierce Birthplace: Amherst County Occupation: Farmer Consort of: Jeff Wright Informant: Jeff Wright Relationship: Husband	

Appendix: Amherst County, Virginia, Death Records

Book/Page	Date	Decedent	Information	Identification
	1879/06/12	Catherine Wright	Place: Amherst County, Virginia Race: White Sex: Female Age: 63 Place: Amherst County Cause: Consumption Parents: Bart & Nancy Whitehead Birthplace: Amherst Occupation: Farmer Consort of: Daniel S. Wright Informant: Danl. S. Wright Relationship: Husband	Catherine (Whitehead) Wright, wife of 1882 Daniel L. Wright of Amherst County, a son of 1850 Jesse Wright of Nelson County, grandson of 1799 Benjamin Wright of Amherst County, and great grandson of 1767 Francis Wright of Amherst County
	1879/12/00	Edward S. Wright	Place: Amherst County, Virginia Race: White Sex: Male Age: 20 Place: Amherst Cause: Typhoid Fever Parents: Shelton H. & Elizabeth Wright Birthplace: Amherst Occupation: Farmer Consort of: Unmarried Informant: W. H. Wright Relationship: Brother	1879 Edward S. Wright of Amherst County, son of 1862 Shelton H. Wright of Amherst County, grandson of 1873 Jesse Wright of Amherst County, great grandson of 1830 Moses Wright of Amherst County, great great grandson of 1799 Benjamin Wright of Amherst County, and great great great grandson of 1767 Francis Wright of Amherst County

Appendix: Amherst County, Virginia, Death Records

Book/Page	Date	Decedent	Information	Identification
	1880/05/00	Ellis Wright	Place: Amherst County, Virginia Race: White Sex: Male Age: 73 Place: Amherst Cause: Consumption Parents: Jessee & Dicy Wright Birthplace: Amherst Occupation: Farmer Consort of: Sarah Paulina Wright Informant: Joseph P. Camden Relationship: Son-in-Law	1880 Ellis Wright of Amherst County, son of 1850 Jesse Wright of Nelson County, grandson of 1799 Benjamin Wright of Amherst County, and great grandson of 1767 Francis Wright of Amherst County
	1880/06/00	Willie Wright	Place: Amherst County, Virginia Race: White Sex: Male Age: 3 Months Place: Amherst Cause: Teething Parents: Lewis & (Not Stated) Wright Birthplace: Amherst Occupation: Farmer Consort of: Unmarried Informant: Lewis Wright Relationship: Father	1880 William Wright of Amherst County, son of Daniel Lewis Wright, grandson of Benjamin Wright, great grandson of 1830 Moses Wright of Amherst County, great great grandson of 1799 Benjamin Wright of Amherst County, and great great great grandson of 1767 Francis Wright of Amherst County

Appendix: Amherst County, Virginia, Death Records

Book/Page	Date	Decedent	Information	Identification
	1880/06/12	Polly Wright	Place: Amherst County, Virginia Race: Colored Sex: Female Age: 90 Place: Amherst Cause: Cold Birthplace: Amherst Occupation: Farmer Consort of: Unmarried Informant: Jeff Wright Relationship: Son	
	1880/08/00	Mary Wright	Place: Amherst County, Virginia Race: Colored Sex: Female Age: 60 Place: Amherst Cause: Cold Birthplace: Amherst Occupation: Farmer Consort of: Unmarried Informant: Marshall Hudson Relationship: Son-in-Law	
	1880/08/03	Benjamin E. Wright	Place: Amherst County, Virginia Race: White Sex: Male Age: 53 Place: Amherst County Cause: Paralysis Parents: Wm. P. & Helena Wright Birthplace: Amherst Occupation: Farmer Consort of: Mary F. Wright Informant: Mary F. Wright Relationship: Wife	1880 Benjamin Edward Wright of Amherst County, son of 1881 William P. Wright of Appomattox County, grandson of Charles Wright, and great grandson of Robert Wright, Sr. (Campbell County)

Appendix: Amherst County, Virginia, Death Records

Book/Page	Date	Decedent	Information	Identification
	1881/10/17	Emma Wright	Place: Amherst County, Virginia Race: Colored Sex: Female Age: 5 Place: Amherst County Cause: Burn Parents: Jeff & Casy Wright Birthplace: Amherst Occupation: Farmer Consort of: Unmarried Informant: Jeff Wright Relationship: Father	
	1882/04/05	Daniel L. Wright	Place: Amherst County, Virginia Race: White Sex: Male Age: 71 Place: Amherst County Cause: Pneumonia Parents: Jessee & Dicy Wright Birthplace: Amherst County Occupation: Farmer Consort of: Unmarried Informant: C. H. Wright Relationship: Friend	1882 Daniel L. Wright of Amherst County, son of 1850 Jesse Wright of Nelson County, grandson of 1799 Benjamin Wright of Amherst County, and great grandson of 1767 Francis Wright of Amherst County
	1882/06/18	Jesse F. Wright	Place: Amherst County, Virginia Race: White Sex: Male Age: 6 months Place: Amherst County Cause: Whooping cough Parents: Chas. & Dicy Wright Birthplace: Amherst County Consort of: Unmarried Informant: C. H. Wright Relationship: Father	

Appendix: Amherst County, Virginia, Death Records

Book/Page	Date	Decedent	Information	Identification
	1883/02/28	Wm Wright	Place: Amherst County, Virginia Race: Colored Sex: Male Age: 5 months Place: Amherst County Cause: Parents: Hugh & Alice Wright Birthplace: Amherst Occupation: Farmer Consort of: Unmarried Informant: Hugh Wright Relationship: Father	
	1884/10/19	Herbert Wright	Place: Amherst County, Virginia Race: White Sex: Male Age: 4 Place: Amherst County Cause: Fever Parents: Sam & Jane Wright Birthplace: Amherst	
	1885/08/15	Nancy Wright	Place: Amherst County, Virginia Race: White Sex: Female Age: 49 Place: Amherst County Cause: Inflammatory Rheumatism Parents: Jas. & Betsy Thompson Birthplace: Amherst Occupation: Farmer Consort of: D. S. Wright Informant: D. S. Wright Relationship: Husband	Nancy (Thompson) Wright, wife of Daniel Lewis Wright, a son of Benjamin Wright, grandson of 1830 Moses Wright of Amherst County, great grandson of 1799 Benjamin Wright of Amherst County, and great great grandson of 1767 Francis Wright of Amherst County

Appendix: Amherst County, Virginia, Death Records

Book/Page	Date	Decedent	Information	Identification
	1886/05/04	Nathan Wright	Place: Amherst County, Virginia Race: White Sex: Male Age: 35 Place: Amherst Cause: Fever Parents: Charles & Sally Wright Birthplace: Amherst	1886 Nathaniel Wright of Amherst County, son of 1882 Charles H. Wright of Amherst County, grandson of Benjamin Wright, great grandson of 1830 Moses Wright of Amherst County, great great grandson of 1799 Benjamin Wright of Amherst County, and great great great grandson of 1767 Francis Wright of Amherst County
	1886/10/26	Merideth Wright	Place: Amherst County, Virginia Race: Colored Sex: Male Age: 30 Place: Amherst County Cause: Fall in Mine Parents: Jeff & Sarah Wright Birthplace: Amherst Occupation: Farmer Consort of: Susan Wright Informant: Susan Wright Relationship: Wife	
	1888/09/03	John Wright	Place: Amherst County, Virginia Race: Colored Sex: Male Age: 4 Place: Amherst Cause: Pneumonia Parents: John & Emma Wright Birthplace: Amherst Informant: John Wright Relationship: Father	

0413(031807)

Appendix: Amherst County, Virginia, Death Records

Book/Page	Date	Decedent	Information	Identification
	1890/08/04	Alex Wright	Place: Amherst County, Virginia Race: Colored Sex: Male Age: 17 Place: Amherst Cause: Blood Poison Parents: Peter & Anna Wright Birthplace: Amherst County Informant: Anna Wright Relationship: Mother	
	1894/06/18	Tobe Wright	Place: Amherst County, Virginia Race: White Sex: Male Age: 67 Place: Amherst	1894 David Staples Wright of Amherst County, son of 1873 Robert D. Wright of Amherst County, probably grandson of Charles Wright, and great grandson of Robert Wright, Sr. (Campbell County)
	1895/11/07	Wm. G. Wright	Place: Amherst County, Virginia Race: White Sex: Male Age: 8 Months Place: Amherst, Virginia Cause: Cholera Infantum Parents: C. H. & S. J. Wright Birthplace: Amherst, Virginia Consort of: Unmarried Informant: Father	
	1897/02/02	____ Wright	Place: Amherst County, Virginia Race: White Sex: Male Age: 2 Months Place: Amherst Parents: Ben & Annie Wright	

Appendix: Amherst County, Virginia, Death Records

Book/Page	Date	Decedent	Information	Identification
	1912/04/22	Herman Wright	Place: Amherst District: Temperance File No: 7984 Registered No: 7 Sex: Male Color: Negro Status: Single Born: Age: 21 yrs Occupation: Laborer Birthplace: Amherst Co Father: John Wright Father's Birthplace: Amherst Co Mother: Easter Tolliver Mother's Birthplace: Amherst Co. Informant: F. P. Nelson M.D. Address: New Glasgow, Va Filed: Ap. 24th 1915 Registrar: V McGinnis Cause: ____ Optical Meningitis - probably tubercular Duration: 10 ds Signed: J. P. Nelson, M.D. Date: April 23, 1912 Address: New Glasgow Va Length of Res: Buried: New Glasgow, Va Date of Burial: April 24, 1915 Undertaker: J. W. Shrader Address: Amherst Va	

Appendix: Amherst County, Virginia, Death Records

Book/Page	Date	Decedent	Information	Identification
	1912/07/26	Reginald Wright	Place: Amherst District: Elon Town: Madison Heights File No: 1176 Primary Registration No: 53 Registered No: 223 Sex: Male Color: White Status: Single Born: Apr 18, 1911 Age: 1 yr 3 mos Occupation: None Birthplace: Va Father: James M Wright Father's Birthplace: Va Mother: Mattie L. Drinkard Mother's Birthplace: Amherst Co Va Informant: James M Wright Address: Madison Filed: July 26, 1912 Registrar: Geo S Dodson Cause: Oleo Colitis Duration: 10 ds Contributory: Pertussis Duration: 40 ds Signed: Geo. T. Harris Date: July 26, 1912 Address: Madison Heights Va Length of Res: Buried: Meads Date of Burial: July 27, 1912 Undertaker: N. B. Duiguid Address Lbg Va	

Appendix: Amherst County, Virginia, Death Records

Book/Page	Date	Decedent	Information	Identification
	1912/12/18	____ Wright	Triplet No 1 Place: Amherst District: Court House File No: 12674 Registered No: 33 Sex: Male Color: Colored Status: Single Born: December 17, 1912 Age: 1 ds. Birthplace: Amherst County Father: not known Father's Birthplace: Mother: Signora Wright Mother's Birthplace: Amherst County Informant: Harry Dickerson Address: Amherst Va Filed: Dec 26, 1912 Registrar: W W Gilbert Cause: not known Signed: Harry Dickerson Date: Dec 26, 1912 Address: Amherst Va Length of Res: Buried: Amherst County Date of Burial: Dec 19, 1912 Undertaker: None	

Appendix: Amherst County, Virginia, Death Records

Book/Page	Date	Decedent	Information	Identification
	1912/12/18	____ Wright	Triplet No 2 Place: Amherst District: Court House File No: 12675 Primary Registration No: 50 Registered No: 34 Sex: Male Color: Colored Status: Single Born: December 17, 1912 Age: 1 day Occupation: Birthplace: Amherst County Father: not known Father's Birthplace: Mother: Signora Wright Mother's Birthplace: Amherst County Informant: Harry Dickerson Address: Amherst Va Filed: Dec 26, 1912 Registrar: W W Gilbert Cause: not known Signed: Harry Dickerson Date: Dec 26, 1912 Address: Amherst Va Length of Res: Buried: Amherst County Date of Burial: Dec 19, 1912 Undertaker: none	

Appendix: Amherst County, Virginia, Death Records

Book/Page	Date	Decedent	Information	Identification
	1912/12/18	____ Wright	Triplet No 3 Place: Amherst District: Court House File No: 12676 Primary Registration No: 50 Registered No: 35 Sex: Male Color: Colored Status: Single Born: December 17, 1912 Age: 1 ds. Birthplace: Amherst County Father: not known Father's Birthplace: Mother: Signora Wright Mother's Birthplace: Amherst County Informant: Harry Dickerson Address: Amherst Va Filed: Dec 26, 1912 Registrar: W W Gilbert Cause: not known Signed: Harry Dickerson Date: Dec 26, 1912 Address: Amherst Va Length of Res: Buried: Amherst County Date of Burial: Dec 19, 1912 Undertaker: None	

Appendix: Amherst County, Virginia, Death Records

Book/Page	Date	Decedent	Information	Identification
	1913/02/17	John W. Wright	Place: Amherst District: Court House City: Riverville File No: 2665 Primary Registration No: 50 Registered No: 15 Sex: Male Color: White Status: Married Born: Jan 10, 1853 Age: 60 yrs 1 mo 6 ds Occupation: Carpenter Birthplace: Appomattox co Father: Ben F. Wright Father's Birthplace: Appomattox Mother: Mary F. Rogers Mother's Birthplace: Appomattox Co Va Informant: G. L. Hissan Address: Riverville Va Filed: Feb 18, 1913 Registrar: W W Gilbert Cause: Valscular hear disease Duration: 10 ds Contributory: Acute Indigestion Signed: W. L. Watts M.D. Date: Feb. 17, 1913 Address: Allens Creek Va Length of Res: Buried: Allens Creek Amherst County Date of Burial: Feb 19, 1918 Undertaker: Freuds Address: Allens Creek	

0413(031807)

Appendix: Amherst County, Virginia, Death Records

Book/Page	Date	Decedent	Information	Identification
	1913/03/11	Hattie Martha Wright	Place: Amherst District: Elon File No: 5142 Sex: F Color: W Status: Single Born: Oct 9, 1891 Age: 21 yrs. Occupation: none Birthplace: Radford Va Father: Edward Jackson Wright Father's Birthplace: Amherst Co Va Mother: Nannie Edward Akers Mother's Birthplace: Radford Va Informant: E J Wright Address: Madison Heights Registrar: Geo S. Dodson Cause: Pulmonary Tuberculosis Duration: 2 yrs Signed: Geo. T. Harris Date: Mar 13, 1913 Address: Modeson Heights Va Length of Res: Buried: Spring Hill Date of Burial: Mar 1913 Undertaker: N. S. Duiguid Address: Lbg Va	

Appendix: Amherst County, Virginia, Death Records

Book/Page	Date	Decedent	Information	Identification
	1913/05/23	Pearl Wright	Place: Amherst File No: 13164 Sex: Female Color: Colored Status: Married Born: 1890 Age: 23 yrs Occupation: Housewife Birthplace: Amherst County Father: George Watkins Father's Birthplace: Amherst County Mother: Melie Pollard Mother's Birthplace: Amherst County Informant: Edward Wright Address: Clifford Filed: June 27th 1913 Registrar: V Mc____ Cause: Gunshot wound of thorax addicental Signed: Edward Dandridge M.D. Date: May 24, 1913 Address: Amherst, Va Length of Res: Buried: Clifford Va. Date of Burial: May 25, 1913 Undertaker: Wash Shrader Address: Amherst Va	

Appendix: Amherst County, Virginia, Death Records

Book/Page	Date	Decedent	Information	Identification
	1914/02/09	Allie Lu Wright	Place: Amherst District: Elon File No: 2601 Primary Registration No: 53 Registered No: 7 Sex: F Color: W Status: Single Born: March 11, 1895 Age: 19 yrs Occupation: none Birthplace: Amherst Co Va Father: Edward Jackson Wright Father's Birthplace: Amherst Co Va Mother: Nannie Akers Mother's Birthplace: Pulaski Co Va Informant: E J Wright Address: Madison Ht Registrar: Geo S Dodson Cause: Pulmonary Tuberculosis Duration: 2 mos Signed: Geo T. Harris M.D. Date: Feb 9, 1914 Address: Madison Heights Length of Res: Buried: Spring Hill Date of Burial: Feb 10, 1914 Undertaker: N D Diuguid Address: Lbg Va	

Appendix: Amherst County, Virginia, Death Records

Book/Page	Date	Decedent	Information	Identification
	1914/07/01	Lester Arnold Wright	Place: Amherst District: Elon File No: 15367 Sex: M Color: W Status: Single Born: July 14, 1913 Age: 11 mos Occupation: none Birthplace: Amherst Co Va Father: James Monroe Wright Father's Birthplace: Appomattox Co Va Mother: Mattie Lee Drinkard Mother's Birthplace: Amherst Co Va Informant: J M Wright Address: Madison Hts Registrar: Geo S Dodson Cause: Meningitis Duration: 1 ds Contributory: Gastro Enteritis Duration: 3 ds Signed: Geo Harris M.D. Date: July 1, 1914 Address: Madeson Heights Length of Res: Buried: Meades Date of Burial: July 2, 1914 Undertaker: N D. Diuguid Address: Sbg Va	

Appendix: Amherst County, Virginia, Death Records

Book/Page	Date	Decedent	Information	Identification
	1914/07/03	Robert Henry Wright	Place: Amherst District: Court House File No: 15352 Primary Registration No: 50 Registered No: 33 Residence in City: 5 Mos 5 Days Sex: Male Color: Colored Status: S Born: Feb 25th, 1914 Age: 5 mos 5 ds Occupation: None Birthplace: Amherst, Va. Father: Arthur Wright Father's Birthplace: Amherst Co Va. Mother: Harriet Dickerson Mother's Birthplace: Amherst Co. Informant: J W. Hutcherson Address: Dearborn Amherst Co. Filed: July 20, 1914 Registrar: W W Gilbert Cause: Flea Collitis Duration: 14 ds Signed: R B Ward Date: July 3, 191_ Address: Amherst Length of Res: Buried: Amherst Co Va Date of Burial: July 4, 1914 Undertaker: J W Shrader Address: Amherst Va	

Appendix: Amherst County, Virginia, Death Records

Book/Page	Date	Decedent	Information	Identification
	1914/09/17	Dan Wright	Place: Amherst District: Court House File No: 20497 Sex: Male Color: Colored Status: Single Born: Dont Know Age: 22 yrs Occupation: Laborer Birthplace: Amherst Co Va Father: John Wright Father's Birthplace: Bedford Co Va Mother: Ema Anderson Mother's Birthplace: Amherst Co Va Informant: M. B. Taylor Address: Colwell Va Filed: Oct 1, 1914 Registrar: W. W. Gilbert Cause: Cystitis & Peritonitis due to blow on abdomen, accidental Duration: 24 ds Signed: R B Ware M.D. Date: Sept 1914 Address: Amherst Length of Res: Buried: Coldwell Va Date of Burial: Sept 18, 1914 Undertaker: J W Shrader Address: Amherst Va	

Appendix: Amherst County, Virginia, Death Records

Book/Page	Date	Decedent	Information	Identification
	1914/10/25	Amy Wright	Place: Amherst District: Court House Registration District: 50 File No: 22653 Primary Registration No: 59 Sex: Female Color: Negro Status: Single Born: not known Age: About 86 yrs Occupation: Inmate of Co. Alms House Birthplace: Virginia Father: not known Father's Birthplace: not known Mother: not known Mother's Birthplace: not known Informant: E F Struelt Address: Amherst Va Filed: Nov 2, 1914 Registrar: W W Gilbert Cause: Senile Gaugreen Duration: 4 mos Contributory: none Signed: Edward Dandridge M.D. Date: Oct 26, 1914 Address: Amherst, Va Length of Res: Buried: Co Alms House Date of Burial: Oct 2, 1914 Undertaker: W. D Burford Address: Lynchburg Va	

Appendix: Amherst County, Virginia, Death Records

Book/Page	Date	Decedent	Information	Identification
	1915/06/04	Rosa Bill Wright	Place: Amherst District: Pedlar File No: 13102 Primary Registration No: 52 Sex: Female Color: White Status: Single Born: June 1, 1915 Age: 4 ds Occupation: None Birthplace: Amherst Co Father: Havey C Wright Father's Birthplace: Amherst Co. Mother: Elizebeth Hamilton Mother's Birthplace: Amherst Co Informant: Mrs John Hamilton Address: Filed: June 15, 1915 Registrar: H T Burks Cause: Convulsions Signed: E M Sandeler(?) M.D. Date: June 4th, 1915 Address: Pleasant View Length of Res: Buried: Amherst Co Va Date of Burial: June 4, 1914 Undertaker: M Pariss Dodd Address: Sandidges Va	

Appendix: Amherst County, Virginia, Death Records

Book/Page	Date	Decedent	Information	Identification
	1915/07/10	Elloiase Wright	Place: Amherst District: Temperance File No: 15504 Primary Registration No: 50 District No: 51A Registered No: 13 Sex: Female Color: Colored Status: Single Born: June 11, 1915 Age: 29 ds Occupation: None Birthplace: Amherst Co Va. Father: Hugh Wright Father's Birthplace: Amherst Co Va. Mother: Sallie Rucker Mother's Birthplace: Armherst Co Va. Informant: Sallie Wright Address: Clifford Va. Filed: July, 1915 Registrar: V McGinnis Cause: Spasms Signed: Mother Address: Sallie Wright Length of Res: Buried: Clifford Date of Burial: July 11th, 1915 Undertaker: Robert Campbell Address: Clifford	

Appendix: Amherst County, Virginia, Death Records

Book/Page	Date	Decedent	Information	Identification
	1916/08/14	Sallie Wright	Place: Amherst District: Temperance File No: 19276 Primary Registration District: 51 Registered No: 18 Sex: Female Color: White Status: Single Born: 1841 Age: 75 yrs 3 mos 10 ds Occupation: House Keeper Birthplace: Amherst Father: Doctor Wright Father's Birthplace: Amherst Co Mother: Nancy Camden Mother's Birthplace: Amherst Co Informant: Chas P Smith MD Address: Lowesville Va Registrar: J J Martin Cause: Tuberculosis Signed: Address: Length of Res: Buried: Date of Burial: Undertaker: Address:	

0413(031807)

Appendix: Amherst County, Virginia, Death Records

Book/Page	Date	Decedent	Information	Identification
	1916/09/10	Nannie Elizabeth Wright	Place: Amherst District: Elon Town: Madison Heights File No: 21807 Sex: F Color: W Status: Married Born: Oct 20, 1970 Age: 45 yrs Occupation: Housewife Birthplace: Amherst Co. Va. Father: James Gowin(?) Father's Birthplace: Amherst Co. Va. Mother: Bettie Viar Mother's Birthplace: Appomattox Co Va Informant: C. W. Wright Address: Madison Heights Va Filed: Sept 12, 1916 Registrar: H. C. Dawson Cause: Colon_ Stomach Duration: 2 mos Contributory: ____illogra Duration: 1 yr 2 mos Signed: G W T. Harris M.D. Date: Sept 11, 1916 Address: Madison Heights Va Length of Res: Buried: Meades Cem. Date of Burial: Sept 12th, 1916 Undertaker: W D Duiguid Address: Lbg Va	

Appendix: Amherst County, Virginia, Death Records

Book/Page	Date	Decedent	Information	Identification

	1916/10/18	Ruth M. Wright	Place: Amherst
			City: State Epileptic Colony
			    Madison Heights
			    P.O. Lynchburg
			File No: 24120
			Primary Registration District: 53
			Registered No: 68
			Sex: Female
			Color: White
			Status: Single
			Born: 21 years
			Age: none
			Occupation: None
			General nature of industry: None
			Birthplace: Damascus Va
			Mother: Mrs. R. M. Sexton
			Mother's Birthplace: Va
			Informant: A. S. Paddy Supt
			Address: Madison Heights
			Filed: Oct. 1916
			Registrar: H. C. Danson
			Cause: Exhaustion
			Duration:
			Contributory: Chronic Epilepsy
			Duration:
			Signed: W. Reid P ____ M.D.
			Date: Oct. 19th, 1916
			Address: Madison Heights
			Length of Res: 2 mos 2 ds
			    All of life
			Disease contracted: Washington Co.
			Former Res: Damascus, Va
			Buried: Glade Springs Va
			Date of Burial:
			Undertaker: J J Hughes Co.
			Address: Lynchburg Va	

Appendix: Amherst County, Virginia, Death Records

Book/Page	Date	Decedent	Information	Identification
	1919/07/24	Alvin A Wright	Place: Amherst District: Temperance File No: 17960 Primary Registration No: 50 Registered No: 8 Sex: boy Color: Col Status: Single Born: February 8th 1919 Age: 6 months 16 days Occupation: None Birthplace: Amherst Co Va Father: Hugh R Wright Father's Birthplace: Amherst Co Va Mother: Sallie Rucker Mother's Birthplace: Amherst Co Va Informant: Hugh R Wright Address: Clifford Filed: July 31 1919 Registrar: V McGinnis Cause: Acute Indigestion Signed: V. McGinnis Registrar Address: Length of Res: Buried: Date of Burial: Undertaker: Address:	

Appendix: Amherst County, Virginia, Death Records

Book/Page	Date	Decedent	Information	Identification
	1919/12/31	Elizabeth Wright	Place: Amherst District: Pedlar File No: 43178 Parimary Registration: 52 Registered No: 7 Sex: Female Color: Black Status: Married Born: Mar 10, 1879 Age: 39 years 7 months 21 days Occupation: Housekeeping Birthplace: Va Father: Peter Gardner Father's Birthplace: Va Mother: Susie Scott Mother's Birthplace: V Informant: R T Thompkins Address: Waricks Va Filed: Feb 10, 1919 Registrar: B. H. Woods Cause: Tuberculosis Disease Contracted: Signed: Address: Length of Res: Buried: Pain Bank Date of Burial: June 1919 Undertaker: E L Smith Address: Pleasant View Va	

Appendix: Amherst County, Virginia, Death Records

Book/Page	Date	Decedent	Information	Identification

	1920/03/28	William Robert Wright	Place: Amherst
			Town: Va. State Epileptic Colony
			    Madison Heights P.O.
			    Lynchburg
			File No: 6697
			Primary Registration No: 52
			Registered No: 7
			Sex: Male
			Color: White
			Status: Single
			Born:
			Age: 19 years
			Birthplace: Virginia
			Father: not known
			Father's Birthplace: not known
			Mother: not known
			Mother's Birthplace: not known
			Informant: A. S. Priddy
			Filed: Mar 29, 1920
			Registrar: H. C. Dawson
			Cause: Terminal Exhaustion
			Duration: 1 ds
			Contributory: Chronic Epilepsy
			Duration: 5 yrs
			Autopsy: No
			Signed: C B Basset M.D.
			Date: 3/30, 1920
			Address: Madison Heights Va
			Length of Res:
			Buried:
			Date of Burial:
			Undertaker:
			Address:	

Appendix: Amherst County, Virginia, Death Records

Book/Page	Date	Decedent	Information	Identification
	1920/10/16	Hiram Wright	Place: Amherst District: Court House Town: Amherst File No: 23516 Primary Registration District: 50 Registered No: 28 Sex: Male Color: Colored Status: Married Paulina Wright Born: dont know Age: 66 years Occupation: Carpenter Birthplace: Amherst Co Va Father: Hiram Wright Father's Birthplace: Amherst Co Mother: dont know Mother's Birthplace: don't know Informant: Ada V Higginbotham Address: 1010 Monroe St Lynchburg Va Filed: Oct 25, 1900 Registrar: W W Gilbert Cause: Softning of Brain Duration: 2 yrs x mos x ds Contributory: none Operation: no Autopsy: no Signed: Edward Dandridge M.D. Date: Oct 20, 1920 Address: Amherst Va Length of Res: Buried: Amherst Va Date of Burial: Oct 17, 1920 Undertaker: J W Shrader Address: Amherst Va	

Appendix: Amherst County, Virginia, Death Records

Book/Page	Date	Decedent	Information	Identification
	1920/11/01	Cynthia Lowe Wright	Place: Amherst District: Madison Heights Town: 408 Main St., Madison Heights File No: 25645 Primary Registration District: 53 Registered No: 84 Residence: No 408 Main St Madison Heights Sex: female Color: White Status: Married Husband: Henry Wright Born: May 31, 1888 Age: 32 years 5 months 1 days Occupation: housewife Birthplace: Nelson Co. Va Father: Thomas Loving Father's Birthplace: unknown Va Mother: Mattie Mix Mother's Birthplace: unknown Va. Informant: Jake Loving Address: 408 Main St. Filed: Nov 3, 1920 Registrar: H. C Dawson Cause: Diabetes Mellitis Duration: 2 yrs. Contributory: Congestion of Lungs Duration: 3 ds Disease contracted: Nelson Co Va Operation: No Test cofirmed diagnosis: Urinalysis Signed: Geo T. Harris Date: Nov 12, 1920 Address: Madison Heights Va Buried: Meades Chapel Date: Nov 3, 1920 Undertaker: W. D. Duiguid Address: Lynchburg, Va	

INDEX

Akers, Nannie, 23
Akers, Nannie Edward, 21
Anderson, Ema, 26
Angus, Eliza, 5
Angus, Pike, 5
Basset M.D., C B, 35
Burford, W. D, 27
Burks, H T, 28
Camden, Joseph P., 9
Camden, Nancy, 30
Campbell, Robert, 29
Dandridge M.D., Edward, 22, 27, 26
Danson, H. C., 31, 32, 35, 37
Dickerson, Harriet, 25
Dickerson, Harry, 17, 18, 19
Diuguid, N D, 23, 24
Dodd, M Pariss, 28
Dodson, Geo. S., 16, 21, 23, 24
Drinkard, Mattie L., 16
Drinkard, Mattie Lee, 24
Duiguid, N. B., 16
Duiguid, N. S., 21
Duiguid, W. D., 31, 37
Gardner, Peter, 34
Gilbert, W. W., 17, 18, 19, 20, 25, 26, 27, 36
Gowin(?), James, 31
Hamilton, Elizebeth, 28
Hamilton, Mrs., John, 28
Harris, Geo. T., 16, 21, 37
Harris M.D., G W T., 31
Harris M.D., Geo, 24
Harris M.D., Geo T., 23
Higginbotham, Ada V, 36
Hissan, G. L., 20
Hudson, Marshall, 10
Hutcherson, J W., 25

James, E. A., Wright, 6
Jeff, Casy, Wright, 11
Jones, T. W., 1
Loving, Jake, 37
Loving, Thomas, 37
Martin, J J, 30
Massey, James H., 6
Mays, E., 2
Mays, Jas S., 2
Mays, Jordan, 2
McGinnis, V., 15, 29, 33
Mix, Mattie, 37
Nelson M.D., F. P., 15
Nelson, M.D., J. P., 15
Paddy, A. S., 32
Pierce, Charlotte, 7
Pollard, Melie, 22
Priddy, A. S., 35
Rogers, Mary F., 20
Rose, Henry, 6
Rose, Winny, 6
Rucker, Sallie, 29, 33
Sandeler(?) M.D., E M, 28
Scott, Susie, 34
Sexton, Mrs. , R. M., 32
Shrader, J. W., 15, 25, 26, 36
Shrader, Wash, 22
Smith, E L, 34
Struelt, E F, 27
Taylor, M. B., 26
Thompkins, R T, 34
Thompson, Betsy, 12
Tolliver, Easter, 15
Viar, Bettie, 31
Ward, R B, 25
Ware, E. S., 5
Ware M.D., R B, 26

Watkins, George, 22
Watts M.D., W. L., 20
Whitehead, Bart, 8
Whitehead, Nancy, 8
Woods, B. H., 34
Wright, A. J., 2
Wright, Alex, 14
Wright, Alice, 12
Wright, Allie Lu, 23
Wright, Alvin A, 33
Wright, Amy, 27
Wright, Anna, 14
Wright, Annie, 14
Wright, Arthur, 25
Wright, Ben, 14
Wright, Ben F., 20
Wright, Benjamin E., 10
Wright, Bettie A., 5
Wright, C. H., 11, 14
Wright, C. W., 31
Wright, Caroline, 7
Wright, Catherine, 8
Wright, Charles, 13
Wright, Chas H., 4
Wright, Chas., 4, 11
Wright, Clarence B., 7
Wright, Cynthia Lowe, 37
Wright, D., 5
Wright, D. L., 3
Wright, D. Lewis, 3
Wright, D. S., 6, 12
Wright, Dan, 26
Wright, Daniel L., 11
Wright, Daniel S., 8
Wright, Danl., 5
Wright, Danl. S., 8
Wright, Dicy, 9, 11

Wright, Doctor, 30
Wright, E., 3
Wright, E. J., 21, 23
Wright, Edward, 22
Wright, Edward Jackson, 21, 23
Wright, Edward S., 8
Wright, Elizabeth, 6, 8, 34
Wright, Ellis, 9
Wright, Elloiase, 29
Wright, Emma, 7, 11, 13
Wright, Francis Jane, 3
Wright, Geo., 1
Wright, Geo. W., 1
Wright, Hattie Martha, 21
Wright, Havey C, 28
Wright, Helena, 10
Wright, Henry, 37
Wright, Herbert, 12
Wright, Herman, 15
Wright, Hiram, 36
Wright, Hugh, 4, 12, 29
Wright, Hugh R, 33, 33
Wright, J M, 24
Wright, J., 5
Wright, James M, 16
Wright, James Monroe, 24
Wright, Jane, 3, 12
Wright, Jas., 12
Wright, Jeff, 7, 10, 11, 13
Wright, Jesse, 6
Wright, Jesse F., 11
Wright, Jessee, 9, 11
Wright, John, 4, 6, 7, 13, 15, 26
Wright, John W., 20
Wright, Julia A., 2
Wright, Lester Arnold, 24
Wright, Lewis, 2, 9

Wright, M. W., 5
Wright, Martha, 1
Wright, Mary, 3, 10
Wright, Mary F., 10
Wright, Merideth, 13
Wright, Moses, 6
Wright, Nan, 2
Wright, Nancy, 3, 12
Wright, Nannie Elizabeth, 31
Wright, Nathan, 13
Wright, Paulina, 36
Wright, Pearl, 22
Wright, Peter, 14
Wright, Polly, 10
Wright, Reginald, 16
Wright, Robert Henry, 25
Wright, Rosa Bill, 28
Wright, Rowland, 4
Wright, Ruth M., 32
Wright, S. J., 14
Wright, Sallie, 29, 30
Wright, Sally, 13
Wright, Sam, 12
Wright, Sarah, 4, 13
Wright, Sarah Paulina, 9
Wright, Shelton H., 3, 8
Wright, Signora, 17, 18, 19
Wright, Susan, 2, 4, 6, 13
Wright, Tobe, 14
Wright, Viny, 5
Wright, W. H., 8
Wright, William Robert, 35
Wright, Willie, 9
Wright, Wm., 5, 6, 12
Wright, Wm. G., 4, 14
Wright, Wm. P., 5, 10

WRIGHT FAMILY

CEMETERY RECORDS BY CEMETERY

AMHERST COUNTY, VIRGINIA

Revised as of August 10, 2007

© 2007, Robert N. Grant
0316(081007)

Introduction To Appendix: Cemetery Records, Bedford County, Virginia

This document is an appendix to a larger work titled Sorting Some Of The Wrights Of Southern Virginia. The work is divided into parts for each family of Wrights that has been researched. Each part is divided into two sections; the first section is text discussing the family and the evidence supporting the relationships and the second section is a descendants chart summarizing the relationships and information known about each individual.

The appendices to the work (of which this document is one) present source records for persons named Wright by county and by type of record with the identification of the person named and their Wright ancestors to the extent known.

The source for the records listed in this appendix is the following:

1) Gravestone Inscriptions in Amherst County Virginia, compiled by Amherst County Museum & Historical Society, Amherst, Virginia, 1999.

The identification of a person or their ancestor by year and county indicates their year of death and county of residence at death. For example, "1763 Thomas Wright of Bedford County" indicates that this was the Thomas Wright who died in 1763 in Bedford County. If no state is listed after the county, the state is Virginia; counties in states other than Virginia will have a state listed after the county, as in "1876 William S. Wright of Highland County, Ohio".

A parenthetical after the name indicates an identification of the person when a place of death is not yet known, as in "John Wright (Goochland County Carpenter)". A county in parentheses after the name indicates the county with which that person was most identified when no evidence of the place of death has yet been found, as in "Grief Wright (Bedford County)".

All or portions of the text and descendants charts for each Wright family identified are available from the author:

Robert N. Grant
15 Campo Bello Court   (H) 650-854-0895
Menlo Park, California 94025   (O) 650-614-3800

This is a work in process and I would be most interested in receiving additional information about any of the persons identified in these records in order to correct any errors or expand on the information given.

0316(073007)

Appendix: Amherst County, Virginia, Cemetery Records

Name	Birth Date	Death Date	Other Information	Cemetery	Identification
Charles H. Wright	1849/08/10	1947/03/27		Alhambra Cemetery Rt. 60 West; Rt. 778 six miles to Rt. 666, 9.8 miles to Rt. 827, left on Rt. 827, 3.5 miles to cemetery	1941 Charles Henry Wright of Amherst County, son of David S. Wright
____ Wright		1928/06/14		Alhambra Cemetery Rt. 60 West; Rt. 778 six miles to Rt. 666, 9.8 miles to Rt. 827, left on Rt. 827, 3.5 miles to cemetery	
Nannie Wright	1850/12/00	1925/05/25		Alhambra Cemetery Rt. 60 West; Rt. 778 six miles to Rt. 666, 9.8 miles to Rt. 827, left on Rt. 827, 3.5 miles to cemetery	
Susan J. Wright	1848/10/30	1929/02/24		Alhambra Cemetery Rt. 60 West; Rt. 778 six miles to Rt. 666, 9.8 miles to Rt. 827, left on Rt. 827, 3.5 miles to cemetery	Susannah Josephine (Wright) (Myers) Wright, daughter of 1870 William Wright of Amherst County, granddaughter of 1850 Jesse Wright of Nelson County, great granddaughter of 1799 Benjamin Wright of Amherst County, and great great granddaughter of 1767 Francis Wright of Amherst County
E. M. O. Wright		1869/00/00		Alhambra Cemetery Rt. 60 West; Rt. 778 six miles to Rt. 666, 9.8 miles to Rt. 827, left on Rt. 827, 3.5 miles to cemetery	
Burnard R. Wright	1876/06/00	1881/11/21		Asberry (Asbury) Church Cemetery U.S. 60 west to Coffee Town Rd (634)	

Appendix: Amherst County, Virginia, Cemetery Records

Name	Birth Date	Death Date	Other Information	Cemetery	Identification
Martha M. Wright	1846/03/22	1919/07/10		Canody-Fulcher Cemetery North on Hwy 151 to Ward Barnes Rd (Rt 665) left turn on Rt 665 for 0.1 mile, on right	
Allen Wright	1928/00/00	1973/00/00		Christian Aid Cemetery Business Rt 29 South, on right	
John William Wright	1895/00/00	1968/00/00		Christian Aid Cemetery Business Rt 29 South, on right	
Margaret Higginbotham Wright	1909/00/00	1977/00/00		Christian Aid Cemetery Business Rt 29 South, on right	
Meredith W. Wright	1888/00/00	1979/00/00		Christian Aid Cemetery Business Rt 29 South, on right	
Olley Wright	1894/00/00	1959/00/00		Christian Aid Cemetery Business Rt 29 South, on right	
Paliene Wright	0000/00/00	1928/00/00		Christian Aid Cemetery Business Rt 29 South, on right	
Virginia R. Wright	1890/00/00	1976/00/00		Christian Aid Cemetery Business Rt 29 South, on right	

Appendix: Amherst County, Virginia, Cemetery Records

Name	Birth Date	Death Date	Other Information	Cemetery	Identification
Alice B Wright	1846/00/00	1888/00/00		Dillard-Hylton Cemetery Rt 29 N about 10 miles; right on Rt 739 one mile	
Henry Clay Wright	1844/04/02	1915/04/11		Dillard-Hylton Cemetery Rt 29 N about 10 miles; right on Rt 739 one mile	1915 Henry Clay Wright, son of 1880 Ellis Wright of Amherst County, grandson of 1850 Jesse Wright of Amherst County, great grandson of 1799 Benjamin Wright of Amherst County, and great great grandson of 1767 Francis Wright of Amherst County
Robert D, CSA	0000/00/00	0000/00/00		Dillard-Hylton Cemetery Rt 29 N about 10 miles; right on Rt 739 one mile	
Annie Elizabeth Dodd Wright	1864/02/14	1953/01/19	Wife of Benjamin W. Wright	El Bethel United Methodist Church West from Amherst Circle, 11.7 miles left on Rt. 635; 2.2 miles to church on left side of road	Annie Elizabeth (Dodd) Wright, wife of 1937 Benjamin Washington Wright of Amherst County, a son of 1914 Henry Talley Wright of Amherst County and grandson of William Wright (Hanover County Tailor)
Benjamin Washington Wright	1851/03/14	1937/02/17		El Bethel United Methodist Church West from Amherst Circle, 11.7 miles left on Rt. 635; 22 miles to church on left side of road	1937 Benjamin Washington Wright of Amherst County, son of 1914 Henry Talley Wright of Amherst County and grandson of William Wright (Hanover County Tailor)
Elizabeth H. Wright	1893/07/11	1982/09/25		El Bethel United Methodist Church West from Amherst Circle, 11.7 miles left on Rt. 635; 22 miles to church on left side of road	

Appendix: Amherst County, Virginia, Cemetery Records

Name	Birth Date	Death Date	Other Information	Cemetery	Identification
Ester H. Wright	1895/10/31	1930/10/31		El Bethel United Methodist Church West from Amherst Circle, 11.7 miles left on Rt. 635; 22 miles to church on left side of road	
Harvey C. Wright	1893/04/10	1978/12/31		El Bethel United Methodist Church West from Amherst Circle, 11.7 miles left on Rt. 635; 22 miles to church on left side of road	
Mary E. (Wright) Camden	1818/04/09	1911/11/27	Wife of Joseph P. Camden	Fulcher at Lowesville Cemetery Intersection of Woodson Rd (666) and Little Piney (629)	Mary E. (Wright) Camden, daughter of 1880 Ellis Wright of Amherst County, granddaughter of 1850 Jesse Wright of Nelson County, great granddaughter of 1799 Benjamin Wright of Amherst County, and great great granddaughter of 1767 Francis Wright of Amherst County
Charles Taylor Wright	1893/00/00	1962/00/00		Harewood Cemetery near Lowesville, Virginia in Nelson Co. Hwy 151 N to Rt 778 (left) to Rt 676 (right) to Rt 677 (left) to end	
Clarence J. Wright	1898/04/11	1967/12/26		Harewood Cemetery near Lowesville, Virginia in Nelson Co. Hwy 151 N to Rt 778 (left) to Rt 676 (right) to Rt 677 (left) to end	

Appendix: Amherst County, Virginia, Cemetery Records

Name	Birth Date	Death Date	Other Information	Cemetery	Identification
Lillian P. Wright	1901/06/13	1983/12/31		Harewood Cemetery near Lowesville, Virginia in Nelson Co. Hwy 151 N to Rt 778 (left) to Rt 676 (right) to Rt 677 (left) to end	
Charles W. Wright	1856/05/18	1935/04/18		Mead Cemetery at Madison Heights 1767-1834 Rt. 29 to Rt. 622 on south side of road	Charles W. Wright, son of 1880 Benjamin Edward Wright of Amherst County, grandson of 1881 William P. Wright of Appomattox County, great grandson of Charles Wright, and great great grandson of Robert Wright, Sr., (Campbell County)
Mary E. Wright	1832/07/18	1918/06/22	Wife of B E Wright	Mead Cemetery at Madison Heights 1767-1834 Rt. 29 to Rt. 622 on south side of road	Mary Francis (Rogers) Wright, wife of 1880 Benjamin Edward Wright of Amherst County, a son of 1881 William P. Wright of Appomattox County, grandson of Charles Wright, and great grandson of Robert Wright, Sr., (Campbell County)
Edd Lee Wright	1865/05/04	1943/05/02		Mt. Pleasant United Methodist Church US 60 West to Rt 631 turn right Rt 631 to Rt 617 turn right	1943 Edward Lee Wright of Amherst County, son of Daniel Lewis Wright, grandson of Benjamin Wright, great grandson of 1830 Moses Wright of Amherst County, great great grandson of 1799 Benjamin Wright of Amherst County, and great great great grandson of 1767 Francis Wright of Amherst County

Appendix: Amherst County, Virginia, Cemetery Records

Name	Birth Date	Death Date	Other Information	Cemetery	Identification
Hamilton Signora Wright	1866/05/18	1950/04/13		Mt. Pleasant United Methodist Church US 60 West to Rt 631 turn right Rt 631 to Rt 617 turn right	Signora May (Hamilton) Wright, wife of Edward Lee Wright of Amherst County, a son of Daniel Lewis Wright, grandson of Benjamin Wright, great grandson of 1830 Moses Wright of Amherst County, great great grandson of 1799 Benjamin Wright of Amherst County, and great great great grandson of 1767 Francis Wright of Amherst County
Houston G. Wright	1901/10/27	1978/10/19		Mt. Pleasant United Methodist Church US 60 West to Rt 631 turn right Rt 631 to Rt 617 turn right	
H. T. Wright	1817/02/27	1914/03/28		Mt. Pleasant United Methodist Church US 60 West to Rt 631 turn right Rt 631 to Rt 617 turn right	1914 Henry Talley Wright of Amherst County, son of William Wright (Hanover County Tailor)
Violet J. Wright	1924/07/14	0000/00/00		Mt. Pleasant United Methodist Church US 60 West to Rt 631 turn right Rt 631 to Rt 617 turn right	
B. B. Wright	1925/06/01	1925/06/17		Rose Lane Cemetery US 29 S Business to Colony Rd (210), left to Rose Chapel and Rose Lane on left - 0.1 mile to end	

Appendix: Amherst County, Virginia, Cemetery Records

Name	Birth Date	Death Date	Other Information	Cemetery	Identification
Alice Wright	1909/00/00	1983/00/00		St Peter's Baptist Church Rt 29 north 3 miles; left on Rt 151 2 to 3 miles to Church on left	
Bessie Wright	1887/00/00	1975/00/00		St Peter's Baptist Church Rt 29 north 3 miles; left on Rt 151 2 to 3 miles to Church on left	
Eugene Wright Sr.	1907/00/00	1983/00/00		St Peter's Baptist Church Rt 29 north 3 miles; left on Rt 151 2 to 3 miles to Church on left	
Rev Hiram Wright	1917/06/08	1971/06/08		St Peter's Baptist Church Rt 29 north 3 miles; left on Rt 151 2 to 3 miles to Church on left	
Mary Wright	0000/00/00	0000/00/00		St Peter's Baptist Church Rt 29 north 3 miles; left on Rt 151 2 to 3 miles to Church on left	
Thomas N. Wright	0000/00/00	0000/00/00		St Peter's Baptist Church Rt 29 north 3 miles; left on Rt 151 2 to 3 miles to Church on left	
Eva B. Wright	1892/05/11	1913/03/16		St Stephens Baptist Church Graveyard Rt 29 north, right on Rt 610, left on Rt 708 across railroad bridge onto Rt 739, right on Rt 657, one mile to Church	

Appendix: Amherst County, Virginia, Cemetery Records

Name	Birth Date	Death Date	Other Information	Cemetery	Identification
George M. Wright	1878/12/21	1940/11/07		St Stephens Baptist Church Graveyard Rt 29 north, right on Rt 610, left on Rt 708 across railroad bridge onto Rt 739, right on Rt 657, one mile to Church	
Lily Wright	1882/01/21	1918/03/22		St Stephens Baptist Church Graveyard Rt 29 north, right on Rt 610, left on Rt 708 across railroad bridge onto Rt 739, right on Rt 657, one mile to Church	
Lillie Belle	1875/10/08	1957/09/16		St Stephens Baptist Church Graveyard Rt 29 north, right on Rt 610, left on Rt 708 across railroad bridge onto Rt 739, right on Rt 657, one mile to Church	

INDEX

Robert D, CSA, 3
Belle, Lillie, 8
Camden, Mary E. (Wright), 4
Wright, Alice, 7
Wright, Alice B, 3
Wright, Allen, 2
Wright, Annie Elizabeth Dodd, 3
Wright, B. B., 6
Wright, Benjamin Washington, 3
Wright, Bessie, 7
Wright, Burnard R., 1
Wright, Charles H., 1
Wright, Charles Taylor, 4
Wright, Charles W., 5
Wright, Clarence J., 4
Wright, E. M. O., 1
Wright, Edd Lee, 5
Wright, Elizabeth H., 3
Wright, Ester H., 4
Wright, Eva B., 7
Wright Sr., Eugene, 7
Wright, George M., 8
Wright, H. T., 6
Wright, Hamilton Signora, 6
Wright, Harvey C., 4
Wright, Henry Clay, 3
Wright, Houston G., 6
Wright, John William, 2
Wright, Lillian P., 5
Wright, Lily, 8
Wright, Margaret Higginbotham, 2
Wright, Martha M., 2
Wright, Mary, 7
Wright, Mary E., 5
Wright, Meredith W., 2
Wright, Nannie, 1
Wright, Olley, 2

Wright, Paliene, 2
Wright, Rev Hiram, 7
Wright, Susan J., 1
Wright, Thomas N., 7
Wright, Violet J., 6
Wright, Virginia R., 2

WRIGHT FAMILY

PROBATE RECORDS

1761-1900

AMHERST COUNTY, VIRGINIA

Revised as of July 28, 2007

© 2007, Robert N. Grant
0126(072807)

Introduction To Appendix: Probate Records for Amherst County, Virginia

This document is an appendix to a larger work titled <u>Sorting Some Of The Wrights Of Southern Virginia</u>. The work is divided into parts for each family of Wrights that has been researched. Each part is divided into two sections; the first section is text discussing the family and the evidence supporting the relationships and the second section is a descendants chart summarizing the relationships and information known about each individual.

The appendices to the work (of which this document is one) present source records for persons named Wright by county and by type of record with the identification of the person named and their Wright ancestors to the extent known.

The sources for the records listed in this appendix are the following:

1) Amherst County, Virginia, Probate Records, available from the Clerk of the Circuit Court, P.O. Box 462, Amherst, Virginia 24521.

2) <u>The Wills Of Amherst County, Virginia, 1761-1865</u>, by The Rev. Bailey Fulton Davis, Southern Historical Press, Inc., c/o The Rev. Silas Emmett Lucas, Jr., P.O. Box 738, Easley, South Carolina 29641-0738, 1985.

3) <u>Amherst County, Virginia, Courthouse Miniatures, An Abstract Of All A Items In Wills From 1761 To 1919 And A Marriages From 1801 To 1854 Of Amherst County, Virginia</u>, compiled by Bailey Fulton Davis, Amherst Courthouse, Virginia, 1961.

4) <u>Amherst County, Virginia, Courthouse Miniatures, An Abstract Of All Items In Will Books 1761-1919 For the B Section</u>, compiled by Bailey Fulton Davis, Amherst Courthouse, Virginia, 1962.

5) <u>Amherst County, Virginia, Courthouse Miniatures, An Abstract Of All Items In Will Books 1761-1919 Dealing With Persons Whose Last Names Begin With The Letter C</u>, compiled by Bailey Fulton Davis, 1964.

6) <u>Amherst County, Virginia, Courthouse Miniatures, An Abstract Of All Names In D Section Of Alphabet In Will Books Of Amherst County, Va. 1761-1919</u>, compiled by Bailey Fulton Davis, Amherst Courthouse, Virginia, 1964.

7) <u>Amherst County, Virginia, Courthouse Miniatures, An Abstract Of All Those Items Dealing With Persons With Last Names Beginning With E, F, G, And I In Will Books 1761-1919</u>, compiled by Bailey Fulton Davis, 1964.

8) <u>Amherst County, Virginia, Courthouse Miniatures, An Abstract Of All Those Items Dealing In Will Books 1761-1919 For The H Section</u>, compiled by Bailey Fulton Davis, Amherst, Virginia, 1964.

The identification of a person or their ancestor by year and county indicates their year of death and county of residence at death. For example, "1763 Thomas Wright of Bedford County" indicates that this was the Thomas Wright who died in 1763 in Bedford County. If no state is listed after the county, the state is Virginia; counties in states other than Virginia will have a state listed after the county, as in "1876 William S. Wright of Highland County, Ohio".

A parenthetical after the name indicates an identification of the person when a place of death is not yet known, as in "John Wright (Goochland County Carpenter)". A county in parentheses after the name indicates the county with which that person was most identified when no evidence of the place of death has yet been found, as in "Grief Wright (Bedford County)".

All or portions of the text and descendants charts for each Wright family identified are available from the author:

Robert N. Grant
15 Campo Bello Court   (H) 650-854-0895
Menlo Park, California 94025   (O) 650-614-3800

This is a work in progress and I would be most interested in receiving additional information about any of the persons identified in these records in order to correct any errors or expand on the information given.

Appendix: Amherst County, Virginia, Probate Records

Book/Page		Date	Decedent	Document	Identification
01	110	1767/09/07	Francis Wright	Will	1767 Francis Wright of Amherst County
01	120	1768/05/02	Francis Wright	Inventory	1767 Francis Wright of Amherst County
01	360	1777/07/07	Augustine Wright	Administrators' Bonds	1776 Augustine Wright of Amherst County
01	378	1777/08/10	Augustine Wright	Inventory	1776 Augustine Wright of Amherst County
03	504	1799/_/_	Augustine Wright	Division	1776 Augustine Wright of Amherst County
03	554	1799/10/21	Benjamin Wright	Will	1799 Benjamin Wright of Amherst County, son of 1767 Francis Wright of Amherst County
03	574	1800/01/11	Benjamin Wright	Inventory	1799 Benjamin Wright of Amherst County, son of 1767 Francis Wright of Amherst County
04	023	1801/10/15	Benjamin Wright	Exors a/c	1799 Benjamin Wright of Amherst County, son of 1767 Francis Wright of Amherst County
04	151	1804/06/18	Jourdan Wright	Inventory	1804 Jordan Wright of Amherst County, son of Parmenos Wright
04	286	1799/10/21	Benjamin Wright	Exors Bond	1799 Benjamin Wright of Amherst County, son of 1767 Francis Wright of Amherst County
04	383	1804/06/19	Jordan Wright	Administrators' Bond	1804 Jordan Wright of Amherst County, son of Parmenos Wright
04	397	1805/02/18	Richard Wright	Administrators' Bond	1805 Richard Wright of Amherst County, son of Parmenos Wright
04	465	1807/09/21	Isaac Wright	Will	1807 Isaac Wright of Amherst County, son of 1767 Francis Wright of Amherst County
04	491	1807/12/21	Nelson Wright	Guardian Bonds	Nelson Wright, son of 1807 Isaac Wright of Amherst County, and grandson of 1767 Francis Wright of Amherst County
04	495	1808/01/18	Isaac Wright	Administrators' Bond	1807 Isaac Wright of Amherst County, son of 1767 Francis Wright of Amherst County
04	515	1808/02/29	Isaac Wright	Inventory	1807 Isaac Wright of Amherst County, son of 1767 Francis Wright of Amherst County

Appendix: Amherst County, Virginia, Probate Records

Book/Page		Date	Decedent	Document	Identification
06	077	1819/06/15	Richard Jordan Wright	Guardian Bond	1858 Richard Jordan Wright of Rockbridge County, son of 1804 Jordan Wright of Amherst County and grandson of Parmenos Wright
06	603	1825/06/20	Betsy Wright	Guardian Bond	Betsy Wright, daughter of Docia Wright
10	049	1838/09/17	Rhoda Wright	Guardian Bond	Rhoda (Wright) Prose, daughter of Benjamin Wright, granddaughter of 1830 Moses Wright of Amherst County, great granddaughter of 1799 Benjamin Wright of Amherst County, and great great granddaughter of 1767 Francis Wright of Amherst County
12	438	1851/09/15	William Wright	Administrator's Bond	1851 William Wright of Amherst County, probably son of William Wright, Jr., and grandson of William Wright (Amherst County)
12	461	1851/09/26	William Wright	Inventory	1851 William Wright of Amherst County, probably son of William Wright, Jr., and grandson of William Wright (Amherst County)
12	474	1851/09/15	William Wright	Will	1851 William Wright of Amherst County, probably son of William Wright, Jr., and grandson of William Wright (Amherst County)
13	108	1851/11/27	William Wright	Division of Slaves	1851 William Wright of Amherst County, probably son of William Wright, Jr., and grandson of William Wright (Amherst County)
13	125	1852/12/11	William Wright	Administrator's a/c	1851 William Wright of Amherst County, probably son of William Wright, Jr., and grandson of William Wright (Amherst County)
14	497	1857/11/16	Jesse K. Wright	Committee a/c	1855 Jesse K. Wright of Amherst County, son of 1851 William Wright of Amherst County, probably great grandson of William Wright, Jr. and great great grandson of William Wright (Amherst County)
16	175	1862/10/20	Shelton H. Wright	Administrator's Bonds	1862 Shelton H. Wright of Amherst County, son of 1873 Jesse Wright of Amherst County, grandson of 1830 Moses Wright of Amherst County, great grandson of 1799 Benjamin Wright of Amherst County, and great great grandson of 1767 Francis Wright of Amherst County
16	213	1863/01/19	Shelton H. Wright	Inventory	1862 Shelton H. Wright of Amherst County, son of 1873 Jesse Wright of Amherst County, grandson of 1830 Moses Wright of Amherst County, great grandson of 1799 Benjamin Wright of Amherst County, and great great grandson of 1767 Francis Wright of Amherst County

Appendix: Amherst County, Virginia, Probate Records

Book/Page		Date	Decedent	Document	Identification
18	068	1871/06/19	A. J. Wright	List of Sales	1869 Andrew Jackson Wright of Amherst County, son of 1873 Jesse Wright of Amherst County, grandson of 1830 Moses Wright of Amherst County, great grandson of 1799 Benjamin Wright of Amherst County, and great great grandson of 1767 Francis Wright of Amherst County
18	117	1871/09/18	Shelton H. Wright	Accounting	1862 Shelton H. Wright of Amherst County, son of 1873 Jesse Wright of Amherst County, grandson of 1830 Moses Wright of Amherst County, great grandson of 1799 Benjamin Wright of Amherst County, and great great grandson of 1767 Francis Wright of Amherst County
18	344	1873/07/20	Jesse Wright	Curatrix Bond	1873 Jesse Wright of Amherst County, son of 1830 Moses Wright of Amherst County, grandson of 1799 Benjamin Wright of Amherst County, and great grandson of 1767 Francis Wright of Amherst County
19	083	1873/07/21	Jesse Wright	Will	1873 Jesse Wright of Amherst County, son of 1830 Moses Wright of Amherst County, grandson of 1799 Benjamin Wright of Amherst County, and great grandson of 1767 Francis Wright of Amherst County.
19	119	1876/02/23	A. J. Wright	Administrator's Bond	1869 Andrew Jackson Wright of Amherst County, son of 1873 Jesse Wright of Amherst County, grandson of 1830 Moses Wright of Amherst County, great grandson of 1799 Benjamin Wright of Amherst County, and great great grandson of 1767 Francis Wright of Amherst County
20	208	1881/09/19	Elizabeth Wright	Administrator's Bond	Elizabeth (Campbell) Wright, widow of 1862 Shelton H. Wright of Amherst County, a son of 1873 Jesse Wright of Amherst County, grandson of 1830 Moses Wright of Amherst County, great grandson of 1799 Benjamin Wright of Amherst County, and great great grandson of 1767 Francis Wright of Amherst County
20	357	1882/08/04	Daniel L. Wright	Appraisement	1882 Daniel L. Wright of Amherst County, son of 1850 Jesse Wright of Amherst County, grandson of 1799 Benjamin Wright of Amherst County, and great grandson of 1767 Francis Wright of Amherst County
20	358	1882/08/04	Daniel L. Wright	List of Sales	1882 Daniel L. Wright of Amherst County, son of 1850 Jesse Wright of Amherst County, grandson of 1799 Benjamin Wright of Amherst County, and great grandson of 1767 Francis Wright of Amherst County

Appendix: Amherst County, Virginia, Probate Records

Book/Page		Date	Decedent	Document	Identification
20	370	1882/03/20	Elizabeth Wright	Acct Sales	Elizabeth (Campbell) Wright, widow of 1862 Shelton H. Wright of Amherst County, a son of 1873 Jesse Wright of Amherst County, grandson of 1830 Moses Wright of Amherst County, great grandson of 1799 Benjamin Wright of Amherst County, and great great grandson of 1767 Francis Wright of Amherst County
20	383	1882/10/16	Charles H. Wright	Administrator's Bond	1882 Charles H. Wright of Amherst County, son of Benjamin Wright, grandson of 1830 Moses Wright of Amherst County, great grandson of 1799 Benjamin Wright of Amherst County, and great great grandson of 1767 Francis Wright of Amherst County
20	401	1883/01/06	Elizabeth Wright	Accounting	Elizabeth (Campbell) Wright, widow of 1862 Shelton H. Wright of Amherst County, a son of 1873 Jesse Wright of Amherst County, grandson of 1830 Moses Wright of Amherst County, great grandson of 1799 Benjamin Wright of Amherst County, and great great grandson of 1767 Francis Wright of Amherst County
20	470	1883/11/19	John R. Wright	Constable's Bond	1928 John R. Wright of Augusta County, son of 1854 Thompson A. Wright of Rockbridge County, grandson of 1815 John Wright of Prince William County, great grandson of William Wright, great great grandson of 1765 Richard Wright of Prince William County, and probably great great great grandson of 1700 Richard Wright of Stafford County
21	166	1885/06/15	Jno. R. Wright	Constable's Bond	1928 John R. Wright of Augusta County, son of 1854 Thompson A. Wright of Rockbridge County, grandson of 1815 John Wright of Prince William County, great grandson of William Wright, great great grandson of 1765 Richard Wright of Prince William County, and probably great great great grandson of 1700 Richard Wright of Stafford County
21	249	1885/09/14	Charles H. Wright	Accounting	1882 Charles H. Wright of Amherst County, son of Benjamin Wright, grandson of 1830 Moses Wright of Amherst County, great grandson of 1799 Benjamin Wright of Amherst County, and great great grandson of 1767 Francis Wright of Amherst County
21	456	1887/07/18	Nancy A. Wright	Administrator's Bond	Nancy Alexandra (Lancaster) Wright, wife of 1853 John Woodson Wright of Cumberland County, a son of 1838 William Wright of Cumberland County, grandson of 1774 Gerge Wright of Cumberland County, and great grandson of 1769 George Wright of Essex County
21	437	1887/06/20	John R. Wright	Constable Bond	1928 John R. Wright of Augusta County, son of 1854 Thompson A. Wright of Rockbridge County, grandson of 1815 John Wright of Prince William County, great grandson of William Wright, great great grandson of 1765 Richard Wright of Prince William County, and probably great great great grandson of 1700 Richard Wright of Stafford County

Appendix: Amherst County, Virginia, Probate Records

Book/Page		Date	Decedent	Document	Identification
22	225	1888/_/_	John R. Wright	Constable Bond	1928 John R. Wright of Augusta County, son of 1854 Thompson A. Wright of Rockbridge County, grandson of 1815 John Wright of Prince William County, great grandson of William Wright, great great grandson of 1765 Richard Wright of Prince William County, and probably great great great grandson of 1700 Richard Wright of Stafford County
23	001	1889/08/22	Wright & Co.	Trustee a/c	
23	135	1891/12/21	Tommie Wright	Guardian Bond	Tommy (Wright) Abbott, daughter of 1891 Thomas Hix Wright and granddaughter of William Wesley Wright
23	152	1891/12/21	Bettie S. Wright	Administrator's Bond	Mary Elizabeth (Childress) (Needham) Wright, wife of 1891 Thomas Hix Wright, a son of William Wesley Wright
23	153	1891/12/21	Josie Wright	Guardian Bond	Josephine (Wright) Banton, daughter of 1891 Thomas Hix Wright and granddaughter of William Wesley Wright
23	153	1891/12/21	Susan Wright	Guardian Bond	Susan Bell (Wright) Nicholas, daughter of 1891 Thomas Hix Wright and granddaughter of William Wesley Wright
23	154	1891/12/21	Walker Wright	Guardian Bond	Walker Wright, son of 1891 Thomas Hix Wright and grandson of William Wesley Wright
23	322	1891/12/22	Bettie S. Wright	Inventory	Mary Elizabeth (Childress) (Needham) Wright, wife of 1891 Thomas Hix Wright, a son of William Wesley Wright
23	344	1893/02/20	Bartholomew Wright	Administrator's Bond	

INDEX

Wright, A. J., 3
Wright, Augustine, 1
Wright, Bartholomew, 5
Wright, Benjamin, 1
Wright, Betsy, 2
Wright, Bettie S., 5
Wright, Charles H., 4
Wright, Daniel L., 3
Wright, Elizabeth, 3, 4
Wright, Francis, 1
Wright, Isaac, 1
Wright, Jesse, 3
Wright, Jesse K., 2
Wright, Jno. R., 4
Wright, John R., 4, 5
Wright, Jordan, 1
Wright, Josie, 5
Wright, Jourdan, 1
Wright, Nancy A., 4
Wright, Nelson, 1
Wright, Rhoda, 2
Wright, Richard, 1
Wright, Richard Jordan, 2
Wright, Shelton H., 2, 3
Wright, Susan, 5
Wright, Tommie, 5
Wright, Walker, 5
Wright, William, 2

Other Heritage Books by Robert N. Grant

Identifying the Wrights in the Goochland County, Virginia Tithe Lists, 1732-84

The Identification of 1809 William Wright of Franklin County, Virginia, as the Son of 1792 John Wright of Fauquier County, Virginia, and Elizabeth (Bronaugh) (Darnall) Wright

Wright Family Birth Records (1853-1896) and Marriage Records (1788-1915): Franklin County, Virginia, 1853-1896

Wright Family Birth Records, 1853-1896; Marriage Records, 1761-1900; Census Records, 1810-1900, in Amherst County, Virginia

Wright Family Birth Records, 1853-1896; Marriage Records, 1808-1910; Census Records, 1810-1900; Patent Deeds and Land Grants; Deed Records, 1808-1910; Death Records, 1853-1896; Probate Records, 1808-1900, in Nelson County, Virginia

Wright Family Birth Records (1853-1896) and Marriage Records (1782-1900): Campbell County, Virginia

Wright Family Birth Records, Marriage Records, and Personal Property Tax Lists: Appomattox County, Virginia

Wright Family Census Records, Deed Records, Land Tax Lists, Death Records and Probate Records: Appomattox County, Virginia

Wright Family Census Records: Bedford County, Virginia, 1810-1900

Wright Family Census Records: Campbell County, Virginia, 1810-1900

Wright Family Census Records: Franklin County, Virginia, 1810-1900

Wright Family Death Records (1853-1920), Cemetery Records by Cemetery, and Probate Records (1782-1900): Campbell County, Virginia

Wright Family Death Records (1854-1920), Cemetery Records by Cemetery, and Probate Records (1785-1928): Franklin County, Virginia

Wright Family Death, Cemetery and Probate Records: Bedford County, Virginia

Wright Family Deed Records (1782-1900) and Land Tax List (1782-1850): Campbell County, Virginia

Wright Family Land Grants (1785-1900) and Deed Records (1785-1897): Franklin County, Virginia

Wright Family Land Grants, Deed Records, Land Tax List, Death Records, Probate Records: Prince Edward County, Virginia

Wright Family Land Records: Bedford County, Virginia

Wright Family Land Tax Lists: Franklin County, Virginia, 1786-1860

Wright Family Land Tax Records: Amherst County, Virginia, 1782-1850

Wright Family Land Tax Records: Nelson County, Virginia, 1809-1850

Wright Family Patent Deeds and Land Grants, 1761-1900, Deed Records, 1761-1903; Chancery Court Files, 1804-1900; Death Records, 1853-1920; Cemetery Records by Cemetery; and Probate Records, 1761-1900, in Amherst County, Virginia

Wright Family Personal Property Tax Lists: Amherst County, Virginia, 1782-1850

Wright Family Personal Property Tax Lists: Campbell County, Virginia, 1785-1850

Wright Family Personal Property Tax Lists: Franklin County, Virginia, 1786-1850

Wright Family Personal Property Tax Lists: Nelson County, Virginia, 1809-1850

Wright Family Personal Property Tax Records for Bedford County, Virginia, 1782 to 1850

Wright Family Records: Births in Bedford County, Virginia

Wright Family Records: Land Tax List, Bedford County, Virginia, 1782-1850

Wright Family Records: Lynchburg, Virginia Birth Records (1853-1896), Marriage Records (1805-1900), Marriage Notices (1794-1880), Census Records (1900), Deed Records (1805-1900), Death Records (1853-1896), Probate Records (1805-1900)

Wright Family Records: Marriages in Bedford County, Virginia

Wright Family Records: Prince Edward County, Virginia Birth Records, Marriage Records, Election Polls, and Tithe List, Personal Property Tax List, Census

www.ingramcontent.com/pod-product-compliance
Lightning Source LLC
Chambersburg PA
CBHW081134170426
43197CB00017B/2857